Planting a Family-Integrated Church

J. Mark Fox

Planting a Family-Integrated Church

by J. Mark Fox

Antioch Community Church
1600 Powerline Rd.
Elon, NC 27244
(336) 586-0997
markfox@antiochchurch.cc
www.antiochchurch.cc

Planting a Family-Integrated Church
by J. Mark Fox

Printed in the United States of America

ISBN 978-1-60647-963-6

www.xulonpress.com

I dedicate this book to Wally, 'Knocker,' Tim, Gentry, Bill, and all the saints at Cornerstone Bible Church. I am grateful for their help in writing it, and for the elders and deacons of Antioch who have helped us live it! I am also deeply grateful to my wife Cindy, who has walked these 26 years of ministry and marriage faithfully by my side. I praise God for 7 wonderful children and a daughter-in-law who all show Christ's love to me. Thank you Micah (and Kari), Caleb, Hannah, Luke, Jesse, Judah, and Susanna! Most of all, I am eternally grateful to the Lord Jesus Christ who saved my soul, and who gave me a vision for church planting.

I appreciate Todd Cline, Chrissy Hahn, Knocker Gaskins, and Cindy Fox for their proofreading and editorial help.

Table of Contents

Foreword xi

1 What is it? 15
2 How do we get started? 21
3 What happens next? 27
4 Who's going to lead? 39
5 Make an appointment 57
6 Come and join us! 67
7 Where will we meet? 93
8 What's in a name? 99
9 What about women? 103
10 What, no programs? 109
11 Who you gonna' serve? 117
12 What about pastors, pulpits, and property? 125
13 How do we get the word out? 137
14 What does it look like? 143
15 Final thoughts 149

Appendix 1: Articles of Faith 153
Appendix 2: Dealing with Money 159
Appendix 3: "Why Plant Churches" 161
Appendix 4: FIC Survey 175

Foreword

Three pastors got together for coffee one day and found all their churches had bat-infestation problems. "I got so mad," said one, "I took a shotgun and fired at them. It made holes in the ceiling, but did nothing to the bats." "I tried trapping them alive," said the second. "Then I drove 50 miles before releasing them, but they beat me back to the church." "I haven't had any more problems," said the third. "What did you do?" asked the others, amazed. "I simply baptized them," he replied. "I haven't seen them since."

Praise God, that has not been my experience as a pastor. Not the bat problem, but the "disappearing members" problem. Oh, we have had more than our share of people come and go, don't get me wrong. But mostly we have seen good and steady spiritual growth that has produced a healthy church which has reproduced, given birth, and sent out new churches. That's what this book is about: planting new churches out of a healthy church.

There are hundreds of books out there about church planting. Why do we need another one?

I can hear someone asking that as they see this book online or pick it up off of someone's bedside table. You have a valid point. Here's how I would respond. There *are* a number of good books on the market about church planting, and I think you should read as many as you can, especially if you plan to be a part of a church plant now or in the future. This book can be added to that number. But there is another response, too. This is about planting a *family-integrated church*, which is a bit of a different challenge. Planting a family-integrated church is only going to be undertaken by a different breed of church planters, and it requires first that you understand and are committed to the basic principles that undergird such a fellowship. Those will be described in chapter 1.

I am a church planter. Not with the same experience and prowess as those who can boast of planting or taking part in planting hundreds of churches. My experience is really limited to three *intentional* plants. There have been two house churches started out of Antioch, but neither one was a plant. But that's a subject for a different book, maybe one entitled, *How to Start New Churches Without Really Trying*. But I have taken part in three churches that I helped to start on purpose. The first was the church I still pastor, Antioch Community Church, in Elon, NC. Five families formed Antioch in 1987. We started the church as a traditional, program-driven church because that's all any of us had ever known. The story about how God took our little church and turned it upside down is the subject of my first book, *Family-Integrated Church* (Xulon Press, 2006).

In 2007, Antioch helped to plant a new family-integrated church in a neighboring county. Chatham Christian Assembly was largely the product of a church in Raleigh, NC, but we helped by "contributing" two families. Our two families wanted to be a part of a new work, especially one family that was driving 45 minutes to come to Antioch every Sunday. Since this new work was going to be in their county, they jumped at the chance to help pioneer a new church. The elders of Antioch met with three families several times who wanted to pursue this new work. We talked about God's heart for His church. We looked at church planting principles from the Scriptures. We prayed together about whether this was the right fit for them. When it all shook out, there were two families who remained committed to the new plant. We got together with them and the core group from the Raleigh church planting team, and the next thing you know, a new church was born. Though we just assisted in the labor and delivery, we still look on as proud uncles (or…cousins?) who are excited about a new baby in the family. We pray for them and encourage them whenever we can, but they are mostly a direct descendant of another family-integrated church.

In the fall of 2007, God laid another opportunity in our laps, and this time He asked us to be the parents, if you will. There were four families in our church from a neighboring county, each of them driving between 45 and 60 minutes to get to Antioch every Sunday. I began to talk with them about a church plant in their town of Asheboro, NC. They were excited about it and started talking to their friends in Asheboro and beyond. Then one day I got an email from a man who lived in Raleigh and was interested in moving to Asheboro to be a part of the new church plant there! We met for breakfast and a few months later his family began driving more than an hour every Sunday to come to Antioch. We began the process of training elders for this new work in January, 2008, and the church met for the first time on a Sunday morning on June 15, 2008. This book is mostly about the principles and the process God took Antioch through as we gave birth to this new family-integrated church. We still have a lot to learn about being 'parents.' And actually, we prefer to call this new work a 'sister church' rather than a daughter church. More about that later. We are thrilled, though, to see a new church growing and thriving in our midst. Our desire is to have many 'sisters,' to send out as many arrows as the Lord will raise up from within our body.

You know what's really exciting? The exponential growth of discipleship is now taking place with churches. There is a healthy and growing church in Asheboro that will one day send out families and singles to start a new healthy and growing church somewhere else. Then that new church will do the same, while the churches in Asheboro and Elon, Lord willing, are doing it again. In the meantime, these new and older churches will be a part of fulfilling Christ's Great Commission. Now *that* is exciting.

I hope this book is an encouragement to you and will provide you with the necessary tools to plant a family-integrated church, if that is God's will.

To God alone be the glory.

J. Mark Fox
Fall, 2008

Chapter One

What *is* it?

What is a family-integrated church, anyway? I wish I had $500.00 for every time that question has been asked. ☺ Actually, it has been a frequent question, and there are many answers, depending upon whom you're talking to. The simplest definition that I have been able to come up with is this: a family-integrated church is one where the family worships together. That's it. There's a lot more to it than that, but that is the common denominator. When the church gathers on the Lord's Day to worship, we are all together, in the sanctuary, and we all participate together in the service of worship. I love what Pastor John Piper says about this:

> Worshiping together counters the contemporary fragmentation of families. Hectic American life leaves little time for significant togetherness. It is hard to overestimate the good influence of families doing valuable things together week in and week out, year in and year out. Worship is the most valuable thing a human can do. The cumulative effect of 650 worship services spent with Mom and Dad between the ages of 4 and 17 is incalculable.

Lest we all just agree and shock the rest of the known world with how easily evangelicals can get along together, let me suggest to you that there is a LOT more to the question,

"What is a family-integrated church?" Some would say that an FIC is a church that doesn't offer a nursery. We offer one. Others would say an FIC is a church that baptizes infants. We baptize believers. Still others would say that an FIC is a church that doesn't use choruses, only hymns. We use both. Some might even say that a real, *genuine* FIC meets in a home, not in a building. We meet in a building. By the way, isn't a home also a building? Others might say that an FIC is a church filled with homeschoolers but no public or private-schoolers. We have all three (or have had, at various times in our ministry). Some might argue that an FIC will be congregational-led. We have elders who lead. A plurality of them. Some would say than an FIC is a church that does not name any of the elders "pastor." That, uh, would be me. Still others would say that an FIC is a place where the women are not allowed to speak during the service. The women at Antioch do not teach or exercise authority over men, in accordance with 1 Timothy 2:12, but they *are* allowed to speak during the service, to share a praise, a thanksgiving, a testimony. More about that later.

Shall I go on? Or is your head spinning enough already? As I said, there is a lot to discuss. That's why when someone calls us and says, "I am looking for a family-integrated church, and someone told me about Antioch," I don't just burst into the doxology and tell them to come on over and join us. The truth is, we don't really want to be known as "the family-integrated church in Burlington." We want to be known as a church that exalts Jesus Christ, loves His Word, is devoted to doctrine, fellowship, breaking of bread and prayer. We want to be known as a church where the people really do love each other and are really and truly committed to serving Jesus with all their hearts. We want to be known as a church where the people take the Great Commission seriously and want to see the whole world reached with the Gospel and are working to that end. We want to be known as a church where the families are healthy and the fathers are leading and the mothers are helping their husbands succeed in God's calling for their lives. We want to be known as a church where the children thrive under their parents' authority and are being brought up in the training and admonition of the Lord. We want to be known as a church where the families who come in and are not healthy are surrounded by believers who will love them and help them *to* health! We want to be known as a church where singles are rejoicing in where they are right now and using their lives to advance the kingdom as they prepare to be married, if that is the Lord's will for them. Oh, yeah. And we are family-integrated. That helps us to accomplish many of those "want to's" more readily, in my opinion. If we wanted to be the biggest church in town, then we would not be family-integrated. We might also not be many of the other things I listed, simply because most churches on a fast-track to 'mega-status' will sacrifice depth and maturity to get there. Not all, mind you. But most. We are family-integrated, mainly, because we believe that's what the Bible clearly teaches about the church. Think about it with me, for a moment.

Why did Paul write his letters to the churches? So that those letters would be read in the churches, right? He certainly did not expect the elders of each church to meticulously copy each letter they received from Paul by hand and disseminate a copy to each family! This was an oral-based culture, after all, and the people expected to be taught by hearing. Paul wrote each letter and sent them by courier to the churches. Then a leader of the church would stand on the next Lord's Day and read the letter to the congregation. If you can stipulate that for me (to use a legal term), then we can proceed with the argument. If that is so, then it stands to reason that everyone whom Paul addressed in his letters would presumably be present in the church meetings. Right? OK, so somebody get a Bible. Got it? OK, look up Ephesians 6. You will remember that Paul addressed wives and husbands in chapter 5. He gave them both some very important instructions. Now look at whom he is addressing in chapter 6, right off the bat: ***Children, obey your parents in the Lord, for this is right.*** What? Why does Paul put that in the letter, when he knows good and well that the Ephesian church is cutting edge? They have the rockingest children's program in the whole region! People come from miles around every Sunday to drop their kids off at the Ephesus KidZone, where they are absolutely blown away by the stage show, the special effects, the fun, the food, the whole thing. I mean, those kids come out of there *stoked* every Sunday, and it's hard for the parents to get them to even leave the building. They just want to keep hanging with their friends and with their children's ministry arts director. What was Paul thinking? That maybe the pastor would leave the 'big church' and walk all the way over to the 'Dungeon' (that's what the youth pastor at Ephesus named the hang-out place for teens) and read the letter from Paul again? To the kids? They're not going to want to listen to the pastor. He is boooring. He is old-school. He is with the parents, the old people, the ancient ones, the blue-hairs....

No. The fact is, the Ephesian church was family-integrated. Ephesians 6:1 is proof positive that there was no children's church. Same with the church in Colosse (reference Colossians 3:20). There were families and singles gathered under one roof, worshiping the Lord together. For more about this, I would point you to my first book on the subject, *Family-Integrated Church* (Xulon Press, 2006). In that book, I explain more about our biblical reasons for doing church as we do church. Let me close this chapter with another quote from John Piper:

Parents have the responsibility to teach their children by their own example the meaning and value of worship. Therefore, parents should want their children with them in worship so the children can catch the spirit and form of their parents' worship.

Children should see how Mom and Dad bow their heads in earnest prayer during the prelude and other non-directed times. They should see how Mom and Dad sing praise to God with joy in their faces, and how they listen hungrily to His Word. They should catch the spirit of their parents meeting the living God.

Something seems wrong when parents want to take their children in the formative years and put them with other children and other adults to form their attitude and behavior in worship. Parents should be jealous to model for their children the tremendous value they put on reverence in the presence of Almighty God. (**DesiringGod.org, "The Family: Together in God's Presence"**)

Chapter Two

How do we get started?

How do we get started? That's a question I have heard through the phone, through emails, and in FIC conferences. How do we start a family-integrated church? This book is written with the assumption that most who read it are in a location where there is not already a family-integrated church that is healthy and that fits your criteria for what you are looking for in a church. If there is an FIC in your area, then go to it! If it has everything your heart desires, except they don't sing the songs you like or the pastor doesn't preach from the version you prefer, my advice is to go anyway. See if you can plug in there and lay down your preferences if the essentials are not a stumbling block. It may not be possible and you may discover that things you thought were preferences for you (like music styles) are really essentials. You may not know that until you go, so go on in. Go in prepared to serve. Do not go in with an ulterior motive ("It may take a while, but I will be able to change this church. I will separate these people from those choruses…or from hymns…or from the NIV..." or whatever). Go in with the heart to serve, not to be served. If, however, there is no FIC, and there is not a church that is remotely interested in "transforming" into an FIC (which is very difficult but can be done!), or there is an FIC but you simply cannot live with their doctrines or their worship styles, or something else that is an essential with you, then you may need to pioneer a new work. How do you do that? Where do you start?

Where does any church plant start? With interested people. When we planted Antioch Community Church in 1987, there were five families who all had the same desire: we wanted to start a new church together. The church we have planted in Asheboro, NC began with five member families, all from Antioch. These are five families who had the same desire: to start a new church together. They all live in the same city, and they believed that God was calling them to start a family-integrated church there. If there had been a family-integrated church already in that location, these families would most likely have attended it. Since there was not, they drove 45 minutes to an hour, one way, to come to Antioch every Sunday.

If you are in a non-FIC church and there are like-minded people in the congregation, do not start a riot. Do not plan a coup. Simply schedule a meeting with the pastor or the elders and ask about the possibility of being sent out to plant a new work. I have a friend about two hours away who was on staff with a large church in his city. God began to work in his heart and gave him a desire to be a part of an FIC. He went to the pastor and explained his vision. The pastor was not opposed to it, but did not believe it was compatible with the vision of the church he and my friend were serving. My friend asked if he could be sent out as a church planter, and though it took months to prepare for the big day, it did come. There is a new FIC in that area of our little world because a man with a vision began to find others who shared that dream and got something started.

Where do you find like-minded people? The best place is in your current church. Again, do not do this as a stealth operation. Be honest with the leadership of the church you attend. Share your vision with them. Ask them to read something about the family-integrated church and then get together with them to discuss it. If the leadership is excited about the idea, it may be that they will gladly work with you to multiply their ministry and help a church plant be launched that is an FIC. If that is the case, rejoice and be exceedingly glad. Many pastors and elders are too territorial and, to be plain about it, too insecure to allow anyone else to start anything else unless it is under their own control. This is a sad state of affairs and should not be...but it is. So, if your pastor or elders are free enough and secure enough to allow someone to have a different vision and to even help them to pursue it, then praise God. He is at work there. Stay under those elders and work with them through the process. Ask them if you are allowed to share the vision with the church body at large and see who is excited about it. Begin to meet with the people in your existing church who share a vision for an FIC plant. There will be more specifics later in this book about what to read and what to do to prepare for a church plant.

What if there is not any interest in the current leadership of your church to help something new get launched? Then you need to pray. Go over their heads and ask the One who holds the hearts of kings in His hands to change *their* hearts. (Proverbs 21:1) But be respectful. Do not seek in any way to undermine the authority of your current church. Believe me that it will not bear good fruit in your own life and in the life of your church plant! You will be sowing seeds in one season that will come to fruition in another season. Fruit that will make you sick.

If you pray and nothing changes, but God continues to weigh heavily on your heart that you are supposed to do something new, then make one last appeal to the leadership. Ask them to send you out with their blessing. If they will not because they have some question about your own integrity and heart, then stop and listen. God may very well be using them to help you get something straightened out before you leave. As the saying goes, "If it doesn't work at home, don't export it." If there is baggage in your own life, the leadership of the church may be able to see it clearly and be used of God to help you get free, before you drag it into the new church plant and *really* have a mess on your hands!

If you make your appeal and the elders don't have anything to say about you and your character, but they just don't agree with your vision, then ask them to send you out anyway. "God often multiplies through division," as many churches can attest. Paul and Barnabus went their separate ways because they could not agree about taking John Mark along, and that was sad. But now there were two missionary teams out there, not just one. We don't know what happened to Barnabus, but we know John Mark was called for by Paul in his latter days, years after the split. ***Get Mark and bring him with you,*** Paul instructed Timothy, ***for he is useful to me for ministry.*** (2 Timothy 4:11). The church I have pastored for 21 years began as five families left a church without the blessing of the sending body. We had tried every way we knew how to be sent out, but it just wasn't going to happen. Here we are, twenty one years later and giving birth to other healthy 'children,' and the church we left continues to minister to the needs of God's people as well.

Let's say you leave the church without the blessing but with the assurance that God is sending you to start a new work. I would suggest that you come under another church, if at all possible. In other words, seek some spiritual covering so you are not out there like 'Lone Ranger' without anyone to hold you accountable. If there is another church in your area that will agree to pray for you and help you with accountability, then ask them to do just that. If the pastor or elders of this church are willing to meet with the men who are leading your new church plant, then by all means do it. Allow someone else to be a part of the process (from the outside; they will have no controlling interest), if they are willing.

If you have to leave your church without being sent out, and there is no other church in your area that is willing to pray for you and help hold you accountable, then you take the next best thing: you get spiritual partners from other cities to help. I have been asked by a couple of groups if I would be willing to help them, long distance, through the process of a church plant. In none of those cases did I have any power or authority. I was simply an advisor, and mainly one who only spoke when spoken to, although they certainly gave me the freedom to give any counsel that I felt led to give. But I was there, and our church was there, to help as we were needed. The truth is, there are thousands of family integrated churches across the country now, and more being planted every month. There is no reason for anyone anywhere to 'go it alone.'

OK, let's take the next case study. Suppose you are a family who *is* all alone, at least in your church. You have read about the FIC movement and you agree with the principles. Your heart does flips when you think about being a part of an FIC, but there are none in your area. You have talked with other members of your church and there are none who feel and believe the same way you do about families worshiping together. What do you do? Here are a few things to try:

- Contact the homeschoolers in your area to see if any of them have the same vision. As you can imagine, FIC principles appeal to many typical homeschool families.
- Put an ad in the local newspaper about an interest meeting for those who would like to talk about the family integrated church, where families worship together and are not divided up at the door. Pick a neutral spot for a meeting, like a room at the library, and see who shows up.
- Do an internet search for "Family integrated church in __________" (your town) and see if anything

emerges. You will be surprised how many people are blogging about the principles of the FIC, and who knows? You might find out that a family just down the street is having 'home church' (just them) until they can find someone who shares their same values.

- Pray. That's not the last resort, it's the first option. I pray every week, many times a week, that God will bring the people He desires to Antioch. Just last year a man showed up one Sunday and sat in the back. In a conversation with him after the service, I found out that he and his family were moving from San Diego to North Carolina. They wanted to be in an area where they could attend an FIC, but they had never heard of Antioch. They rented a house 45 minutes away, but in his conversation with someone in that community, he heard about our church, came to visit once, and the rest is history. They are a vital part of our fellowship now, and the Lord led them here from 3000 miles away! If He can do that, He can lead you to another family, or four or five others, who have a similar heart for family integrated worship. He is a big God, unlimited in what He can do to accomplish His purposes!

Chapter Three

What happens next?

What do you do now? You have a few families, hopefully three or more, who share your vision for the FIC. The next step is to begin to meet together to get ready for a future launch date. Your greatest goal is to see if the core families can work together and agree together to disagree together about the nonessentials. Did you get that? Just because you have a desire to be in an FIC does *not* necessarily mean that you three (or however many) families can live happily ever after. There may be some ogres in this tale just waiting to show up at the prayer meeting.

If there is a man who initiated your gathering together, the first man who had the vision in the area for an FIC, then he is probably the one who will first articulate the vision he has for what that church will look like and how it will practice the fundamentals of the faith. He needs to come prepared to share his vision at that first meeting of the newly formed 'core group.' This is kind of like a courtship. They say that there are two types of successful courtship: the courtship that leads to marriage, and the courtship that does *not* lead to marriage. It is the same with this vision-casting stage of the church plant. If the original visionary casts his vision and the other families are just not excited about it at all, then there are two options. Hammer out a vision that everyone can agree on, or shake hands all around, thank everyone for coming, and agree that you will go and find others who share your separate visions. Either you agree to continue to track towards "marriage," even if it means a lot of give and take and dying to self and laying down certain expectations...or you agree to dissolve the relationship in the early stages, before hearts become entangled to the degree that it would be an ugly mess to separate.

Let us continue with the assumption that the core group hears the 'founding brother's vision' and everyone seems to agree that it is the same vision that they had. Trust me when I tell you that in the beginning stages, many are willing to say just about anything to make it work. You must not do that. Use spiritual discernment to decide which hill you are going to die on, and be willing to stake your claim there and not be budged. It is much better that everyone come into the relationship with as much grace-seasoned honesty as possible. Like a marriage. I heard someone say years ago that most men and women come into marriage just the opposite of the way they are supposed to. You should approach a potential lifelong spouse with a magnifying glass, trying to see every little flaw, every character deficiency, every potential problem that would make you wish you had never married the person in the first place! Then, once you have resolved yourself to love the person like they are, warts and all, and you say "I do" at the altar, then you take off the magnifying glasses and put on the rose-colored glasses. From then on, you approach your mate with acceptance and love and forgiveness, even to the point that you learn to overlook a transgression (Proverbs 19:11). Instead, what many young couples do is just the opposite. They put on the rose-colored glasses during the courtship, not wanting to even admit to themselves, much less confront their partners, about a potential problem they see in this person they think they "love." Then, when they get to the altar and say the "I dos," the rose colored glasses are tossed in the bushes on the way out of the church, and out comes the magnifying glass. Every flaw, every blemish, every character deficiency that they joyfully overlooked during the courtship is now a thorn in their flesh.

Let me hasten to say that with a potential mate or with a potential church-plant team, we must not have a holier-than-thou attitude. We must do all we can to lay aside pride or a critical spirit and look with God's eyes, not the eyes of our flesh. But this examination process must be done; otherwise, we are in for big trouble ahead.

It is better to never marry at all than to marry in haste and repent in leisure. It is better for the church to never be planted than for the church to become a disgrace and a laughing-stock to the enemies of the cross because just a few months or years down the road the whole thing blows apart. Those first vision-casting meetings could not be any *more* important to the future life and health of the church. Everyone must lay his cards on the table and reveal any expectations or hopes or dreams about this new church plant. If the expectations are radically different, the church will probably not be planted, at least not with this core group. If the expectations are minor differences in 'preferences,' not major disagreements about philosophy of ministry, the core group can probably work towards an agreement that satisfies.

I mentioned a number of issues in the third paragraph of Chapter One that could become deal-breakers. If not at the first meeting, very early into the process of planting a new church, these issues should be discussed:

- Will we use choruses or hymns or both? What type of choruses would not be acceptable?
- Will we offer a nursery? If so, for what ages? For how much of the morning service?
- Will we baptize believers or infants?

- Will we have elders? A pastor? Will the pastor be an elder? Will we be congregationally-led or elder-led?
- Will women be allowed to speak during the service? If so, in what capacity?
- Will there be any programs at all in the church? If so, what types of programs might we allow and under what circumstances?
- Will we adopt a particular creed or doctrine that helps to define what we believe? Which one?
- Will we encourage church membership? If so, how will someone become a member?
- Will we seek to grow as large as possible? Or will we adopt a church-planting vision?
- Will we support a mission program?
- Will we encourage people to give regularly?
- Will we have any full-time or part-time staff? What will their responsibilities be?
- Will we meet in a home forever, or move to a larger facility as the need arises? Or will we start in a store-front or some other rented space?
- Will we ever borrow money to buy, to build, or to renovate?
- And last not but least…what *name* will we give this new church? (I was surprised at the energy and ideas this question generated in our group of five families!)

Now, you may label a few of those questions as "essentials." I would argue that they are all nonessentials (if the Bible does not clearly speak on them and their use in the church), and that good solid churches practice everything imaginable on the scale of possibilities for each question! Each one of these questions, and there are many more that you will bump against as you move ahead as a core group, is a potential landmine. For one brother, whether women can share a testimony in the Sunday morning service would be a deal-breaker. He simply would not go to a church where that is allowed. I have met some of those brothers, and they love the Lord as much as I do, though we disagree on this issue. Another brother would not go to a church where women are *not* allowed to speak a testimony or give a word of praise. I think we, too, have the Spirit of God, to borrow a phrase from Paul. So, the bottom line is that these questions must be addressed and agreed upon (or laid down as a nonessential about which you can agree to disagree), unless you want big troubles down the road. More on women's roles in the church in Chapter 9.

There is a list of what I would call essentials that must be agreed on as well. These are core beliefs that I go through with every potential new member at Antioch. We have a New Members' class and part of the discussion is about what we believe. The essentials, which are non-negotiable, would include the following:

- Salvation is by grace, through faith.
- Jesus is fully God and fully man.
- Jesus is the only mediator between God and man; He is our only hope for salvation.
- Jesus was born of a virgin.
- The Godhead is three-persons, God the Father, God the Son, God the Holy Spirit.
- We believe in the authority and the sufficiency of Scripture.
- We believe in the personal, bodily resurrection of Jesus Christ on the third day.
- We believe in the imminent, personal return of Jesus Christ.
- We believe in eternal judgment for all who have rejected the Gospel of Jesus Christ.
- We believe in the importance of the local church.

That is a sample, but each item on that list is important enough to refuse church membership to anyone who disagrees. It doesn't matter if we disagree about whether people should tithe on their gross or their net or they are 'free to give as they please.' But we disagree on the authority and the sufficiency of Scripture at our peril. It is not a negotiable belief! Neither are any of the others in the list above. I recommend that your core group agree on the essentials of the faith. If those cannot be agreed on completely, there really is no point in continuing the relationship, at least the 'church-planting' part of it, anyway!

With Gregg Harris' permission, I want to insert an entry from his blog at this point. Gregg is one of the elders of Household of Faith Community Church, in Gresham, Oregon. He is a well-known author, homeschool advocate, teacher...but some of you may know him as the father of Josh Harris (author of *I Kissed Dating Goodbye*) and "Rebelution.com" twins Alex and Brett Harris (authors of *Do Hard Things*). This blog entry so well communicates my heart for our church, and helps encourage me when I have been sometimes accused of 'doctrinal mushiness,' because I believe all three of these positions are true and can be held together in balance in a healthy church!

Reformed, Charismatic & Evangelical: Keeping the Fire in the Fireplace!

FOR MANY YEARS the Bible has been treated like a deck of cards. Denominations behave like players in some doctrinal "card game" where each church holds only a few cards in its hand as it competes with other churches for new members. Every church has its own "doctrinal distinctives" or emphases which are often reflected in the church's name (e.g. Baptist, Methodist, Presbyterian, etc.) In addition, churches are grouped into larger camps, based on overarching values (e.g. Reformed, Charismatic & Evangelical).

Such divisions rob every church of its heritage in the whole counsel of God.

Generally speaking, Reformed churches hold tightly to the cards (i.e. the passages of Scripture) that pertain to "the doctrines of grace." They also emphasize the need to guard sound doctrine from error. Charismatic churches hold the cards that relate to the Holy Spirit and His gifts. They emphasize supernatural manifestations of the Holy Spirit. Evangelicals hold on dearly to the cards that teach the Great Commission, personal evangelism and world missions. They emphasize winning the lost to Christ.

Our analogy breaks down of course, because no true church is void of all interest in the doctrines championed by the others. But over time, these three camps have drifted farther and farther apart. Today they seem mutually exclusive of one another. What is worse, as each has over-emphasized and over-reacted to each doctrine errors have occurred on all sides. As each church pushes its favorite truth to an erroneous extreme, the other churches attempt to distance themselves from those errors and all but abandon some key doctrines. "We don't emphasize election here." Or, "We are not 'seeker sensitive.'" Or, "We won't stand for Holy Spirit wildfire." In this way major passages of God's Word are being abandoned to other churches who, in their zeal, distort them and make them the primary basis of their church's identity. By being taught without the balance that comes from knowing and believing the other doctrines, every church loses out.

It Takes All Three!

The situation today requires a Christian to attend three churches just to receive a balanced diet of what the Bible actually teaches— one to enjoy expository Bible teaching and basic Bible doctrine (e.g. a sound Reformed Church), one to experience supernatural ministry (e.g. a sound

Charismatic church) and yet another to be equipped to live the Great Commission (e.g. a sound Evangelical church). As long as every church holds only its own limited denominational "hand," no church is "playing with a full deck." The whole counsel of God has become divided, disjointed and out of balance. Household of Faith Community Church in the Portland Metro Area of Oregon (where I now serve as a Teaching Elder), is an attempt to bring these three camps of Bible doctrine back together in one local church. There we strive to be *biblically* Reformed, *biblically* Charismatic and *biblically* evangelical in order to enjoy the benefits (and avoid the errors) of all three. We want everything that the Bible teaches, but nothing more.

Our Strengths Can Become Our Weaknesses

The strength of the Reformed pastor can become his weakness. He has such confidence in the truth of the Bible and the sovereignty of God that he distrusts the Spirit of God and is fatalistic in his response to missions. He becomes cold and academic in his teaching. He closes all opportunities for God to move with power in the church. He "despises prophesy" as "adding to the Scripture." He "forbids speaking in tongues," dismissing it as "wildfire." He is like a man with a massive stone fireplace made up of sound Bible doctrine. But he would rather sit in a cold, dark, empty house than take any chance that the fire might get out of the fireplace, or that careless guests might damage his stone work. He does not understand that his precious fireplace has been designed by God to safely hold the blazing fire of God's Holy Spirit for the benefit of many yet to be saved.

On the other hand, the strength of the Charismatic pastor can also become his weakness. His confidence in the inspiration of the Holy Spirit can undermine his motivation to do the hard work of Bible study and sound doctrinal preaching of the Gospel. He believes he need only read a passage and "pray through" until he "feels the anointing." Then he steps into his pulpit to serve up half-baked ideas to an ever-enthusiastic, but doctrinally famished congregation. This pastor is like a man who builds a bonfire in the middle of his living room floor. A wonderful stone fireplace stands just a few feet away. But he thinks that any attempt to regulate the moving of the Spirit, to limit the use of tongues in the service or to evaluate the content of a given prophesy, (as the Bible clearly commands us to do in 1 Cor. 14:26-33), would somehow "quench the Spirit." He also presumes upon the Holy Spirit in evangelism, failing to explain what God has accomplished for the sinner through Jesus Christ, not taking seriously the fact that the Spirit of God works through the proclamation of the Gospel to save sinners. Fire belongs in a fireplace.

In yet a similar way the Evangelical pastor's strength can become his weakness. His desire to reach people for Christ is admirable. But when he compromises God's Word and despises God's Spirit in order to get more people to make decisions for Christ, he does everyone a disservice. In his attempts to be "culturally relevant" and "seeker sensitive," he can become ashamed of the Gospel, attempting to offer a Savior who is not Lord. Lacking zeal for sound doctrine for fear that God's truth will turn off the visitors, and lacking faith in the power of the Holy Spirit to convict and convert the lost through the foolishness of the Gospel message, such pastors offer only a diet of short, fluffy, topical messages that produces many false conversions. This plague that we call "nominal Christianity" is seen in the growing number of people who now attend evangelical churches, but who have never been born again, have only a false assurance of salvation, who bear no spiritual fruit, are not zealous for good works and who know very little Bible doctrine.

Such an Evangelical pastor does not understand that without the fireplace of sound doctrine to display God's Truth there can be no knowledge of sin, true repentance, nor saving faith. Without the fire of the Holy Spirit to confirm God's Word with power in the new birth, there will be no lasting fruit. It is the combination of the fireplace and the fire that provides an ideal context for effective evangelistic ministry.

The Balance of God's Truth

In each camp, the remedy is to be found in the doctrines now monopolized by the other two camps. The entire Bible is for the entire church! What has been lost in this situation is the integrity of the Truth itself. The major doctrines referred to by the terms Reformed, Charismatic and Evangelical, interact with one another in dynamic ways that check the excesses of one another and maintain the balance of Truth.

By keeping the fire in the fireplace we create the best possible setting for effective evangelism — a beautiful back-drop of God's power in the confirmation of God's Truth as an expression of God's Love. Here we find God's people showing their love for God by the way they love one another. Here we experience passionate worship toward God that is both "in spirit and in truth," and discover a confidence in the Gospel that allows us to boldly speak God's truth in love.

All of the Bible doctrines monopolized and distorted by the three major camps of Protestant Christianity are found in every Bible. They have always been there. They comprise an integrated whole. One group's misunderstanding or misapplication of a doctrine cannot justify the rest of us in ignoring that part of God's Word. All of God's truths are intended to be understood, believed and obeyed in relation to one another by the entire Body of Christ. Every church is intended to be "a full deck church" with all of the checks and balances in place. HOFCC is an attempt to be just that. Thus far we find the combination to be both refreshing and effective. –Gregg Harris, 11-16-05 (used with permission. Go to http://www.hofcc.org/ for more information and updates on Household of Faith Community Church.)

~~~~~~

If I were starting a new church plant today, I would want to do it with people who believed in all three of these doctrinal positions, or *at least* were not theologically opposed to any one of them! Now, let's move to the next step of forming your core group.

Remember what we talked about in the last chapter? If there is a governing body that is willing to be your covering as you work through this process, that's great. If not, then you will have to do it alone. I met with the five men of the Asheboro church plant for several months. We met once a month for 90 minutes to 2 hours for a discussion about books that I asked them to read. But these five families were also meeting *every* Sunday as part of Antioch Community Church, gathering with the rest of us for worship, for Men's Breakfasts, for special meetings and ministries of the church. These five families were also meeting *every* Wednesday as a home group in Asheboro. This was a critical part of the equation for a number of reasons. First, it began to knit their hearts together as they learned to study the Word together, share prayer requests and pray for one another, and fellowship together. It knit them together also because they spent time laughing, having fun together, eating meals together, and just falling in love with each other. The children were involved in all of this of course (we're family-integrated, remember?), and they too were forging relationships and learning to get along.

The first book that I asked these five brothers to read was *Reforming Marriage* by Douglas Wilson. I always keep copies of that book on the literature table in the foyer at Antioch because I believe it is the best book on marriage I have ever read. We should be getting a kick-back from Canon Press for the number of these books we have ordered! Every family and single who decides to come be a part of Antioch
~~~~~~

is offered a copy, and encouraged to read it. In the case of the Asheboro leaders, I did not suggest they read it: I required it of them. I gave them a handout with a few simple questions on it and then we met a month later to discuss the book. Here are the questions:

1. What did the Lord show you through the book about your marriage (things that are working well, things you need to work on)?
2. What did you learn about headship?
3. What do you not understand that you would like to ask the rest of us about?

When we met for our monthly meetings, it was almost always after church. We met in a classroom in the church building. One of my sons would drive to the closest Subway and buy subs and chips for all 6 of us. The church would pay for this meal. Then we would eat together and talk about how things were going with their home group and with their families. After the meal and some informal talk time, we would get into the discussion about whatever I had assigned them for that day. The men were very open and transparent right from the beginning. I attribute that to the Holy Spirit, most of all. He was working in their hearts to prepare them to plant a precious work of God: a church! I attribute their openness also to the fact that they were spending time together in each other's homes as well, getting to know and trust each other. Like a good marriage, a solid church is going to be a family of people who want to accomplish the same goal…together.

It was clear to all of us after our first meeting that the five men around that table had solid, biblical marriages. They were all growing as husbands, they were all committed to loving their wives for a life-time, and they were all humbled by the awesome truth of God's design for headship. It was time to move into the next phase of training: biblical eldership.

Chapter Four

Who's going to lead?

I was having lunch with some pastors and one of the men leaned over the table and asked, "OK, guys, give me your best biblical argument for having lay elders in your church." I looked around at the other guys at the table and nobody said anything. So I started with, "Acts 14:23, Paul and Barnabus appointed elders in every church. Elders, plural, in every church, singular." Then I went on: "Look at 1 Timothy 3 where Paul gave the qualifications for elders. Look at Titus 1 where he says he left Titus in Crete so that Titus may 'set things in order.' The first thing Paul instructed Titus to do (presumably the first thing of order in a church!) was to 'appoint elders.' Then Paul gave the qualifications for biblical elders. Look at 1 Peter 5," I went on, "where Peter instructs the church elders to shepherd the flock. Look at Acts 20 where Paul knows he is heading to Jerusalem to be arrested and probably lose his life, and he calls for the Ephesian elders to come and meet with him in Miletus. They wept with Paul as he instructed them and as he told them that he would never see their faces again. He met with the elders. Plural. Not with a pastor."

I am of the firm belief that the best biblical model for leadership in the local church is a plurality of elders. For that reason, the first thing I want to do with a group of core leaders of families who are thinking of planting a church together is to see if there are any men among them who are biblically qualified to be elders.

I have not found a better resource, besides the Bible of course, to instruct men in what it means to lead and feed and protect as an elder than the book *Biblical Eldership* by Alexander Strauch. Again, Antioch Church is not getting a kick-back from Strauch, but perhaps we should! I have ordered many copies over the years and given them to men in the church who are being considered for eldership. After the Asheboro men worked their way through *Reforming Marriage*, I had them begin to work on the book by Strauch. I have bought the workbook that is available for *Biblical Eldership* (Lewis and Roth Publishers), written by Alexander Strauch and Richard Swartley. Here are the three separate "handouts" I adapted from the handbook. I gave a copy of each of these to the five men in our church-plant group.

Read pages 1-98 and answer the following questions…

1. "Elders are to protect, feed, lead and care for the flock's many practical needs." (p. 17) If you had to explain this concept to a person who had never heard of the idea of churches being led by 'elders,' what would you say?

2. Which of these four areas do you believe you are best prepared to step into, and why? Which, if any, do you feel ill-prepared for, and what do you need to do to get prepared?

3. Why do you think the church has moved away from the "shared leadership" model that is plainly taught in Scripture?

4. What would you say your "fatal flaw" is? (Talk to your wife about this!) (C.S. Lewis' quote, p. 40)

5. Have you seen the concept of "first among equals" in a church or ministry or group you have been involved with, and if so, how did it work?

6. "For the Bible-believing Christian, the primary example of male leadership is found in the person of Jesus Christ." (p. 52) Would you be able to support, from Scripture, the view that biblical eldership is male? How would you do so?

7. "An elder must be an example of Christian living that others will want to follow." (p. 78) Is there any area in your walk with Christ that you would NOT want the young men of the church to emulate?

8. What do you believe most recommends you to the task of elder (or deacon), based on the biblical qualifications?

9. How important is it to you that the elders maintain unity with one another, and what do you think elders need to do to promote such unity?

10. What other thoughts or insights do you want to share from this month's reading?

That's all of the handout for the first meeting. We discussed each of those questions, and each man came prepared with answers he had written down *for each one!*

At the end of this meeting, we took prayer requests, spent some time in prayer together, set a date for the next month's meeting, and then I gave them this handout to use as a guide:

Read pages 101-180 and answer the following questions…

11. (From Biblical Eldership Study Guide): From your past experiences in working with committees or groups, indicate whether the following statements apply: use **T** for true, or **F** for false. Take time to honestly evaluate yourself before God. Ask your wife or a close friend to help you answer objectively.

___ I act impulsively and dislike waiting for others to make decisions.

___ I generally trust the collective judgment of my fellow team members.

___ I feel genuine concern for the interests and plans of my fellow workers.

___ I often act independently of the leadership body.

___ I make myself accountable to my fellow team members.

___ I work hard to cooperate with my partners in ministry.

___ I share my burdens, fears, and problems with my brothers.

___ I am inclined to carry a grudge.

___ I am easily frustrated by disagreement.

___ I am afraid to speak honestly in a group.

___ I feel free to correct and direct my fellow team members.

___ I actively contribute to discussions and decisions.

___ I tend to be bossy.

___ I am too sensitive.

___ I tend to dominate discussions.

___ I have a hard time apologizing or admitting I am wrong.

___ I love my fellow colleagues.

___ I consciously try to be humble and serve my brothers.

___ I pray for my team members regularly.

Identify your areas of weakness as a team member. Give these weaknesses special prayer attention and peer accountability. Together, focus on how the profound quotation by Paul Billheimer (p. 171) applies to you.

12. What are the three most significant truths (to YOU) that can be learned about eldership from the book of Acts?

13. D. Martyn Lloyd-Jones said, "I defy you to read the life of any saint that has ever adorned the life of the Church without seeing at once that the greatest characteristic in the life of that saint was discipline and order. Invariably it is a universal characteristic of all the outstanding men and women of God...Obviously it is something that is thoroughly scriptural and absolutely essential." (Spiritual Depression, 1965) And J. Oswald Sanders said, "It has been well said that the future is with the disciplined and the quality that has been placed first on our list, for without it the other gifts, however great, will never realize their maximum potential. Only the disciplined person will rise to his highest powers. He is able to lead because he has conquered himself." (Spiritual Leadership, p. 67) Both quotes from Biblical Eldership Study Guide.

    Apply these two quotes to what Strauch said in Chapter 8 (in several places) about the necessity that an elder *labor* and *work hard* to serve the flock.

14. Why do you think it is so rare in churches today that elders are "esteemed very highly in love?" What can we do to encourage that practice at Antioch?

15. Are there other points from the reading this time that you want to discuss?

Once again, we met to discuss these points, making sure that each brother had time to share something about each question. I was especially touched by their vulnerability and openness. Again, after prayer, I gave them another handout and the final instructions regarding Strauch's book:

Read pages 181-295 and answer the following questions…

** These questions are adapted from the study guide to Biblical Eldership.

16. Review 1 Timothy 3:1 and 1 Peter 5:1-2. To the best of your recollection:

    a. When did you first desire to be a shepherd elder?

    b. What sparked your initial desire to be a shepherd elder?

    c. Describe an event or problem that has caused you to doubt your desire to be a shepherd elder.

    d. How intense is your desire to be a shepherd elder?

e. Do you ever doubt your qualifications to be an elder? If so, how seriously?

f. If, at this time, you are not appointed to be a shepherd elder, what should be your response?

17. Spend time with your wife talking about your shepherding ministry and its inevitable effect on your marriage and family. Be realistic about the fact that the pressures of being an elder will put your family at risk. Answer the following questions, with your wife!

    a. Can you be an exemplary husband and also serve as an elder?

    b. Can your wife wholeheartedly support your ministry?

18. Go over the qualifications in 1 Timothy 3 for elder (or deacon). Evaluate yourself with this tool, and ask your wife to make an independent evaluation of you as well. Sit down with her and compare your answers.

    a. A one-woman kind of man:

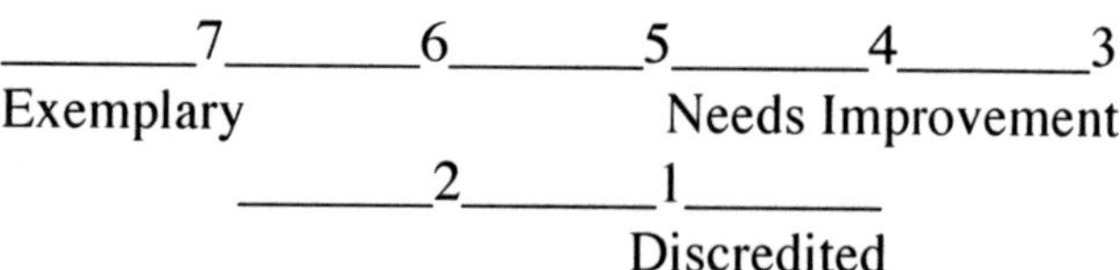

b. Temperate: a self-controlled, balanced man:

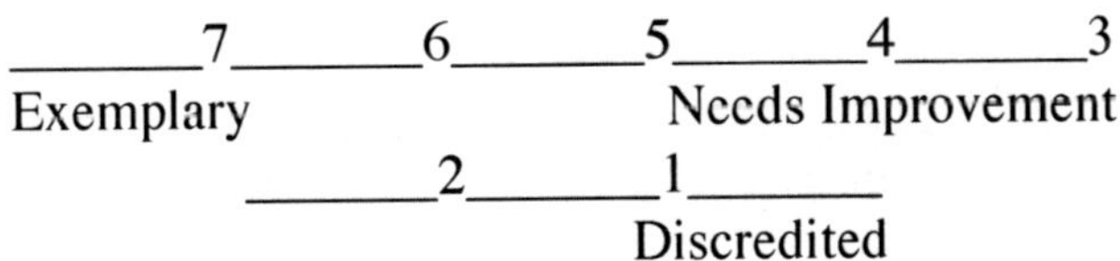
_______7_______6_______5_______4_______3
Exemplary Nccds Improvement
_______2_______1_______
Discredited

c. Prudent: a sensible man, of good judgment and discretion:

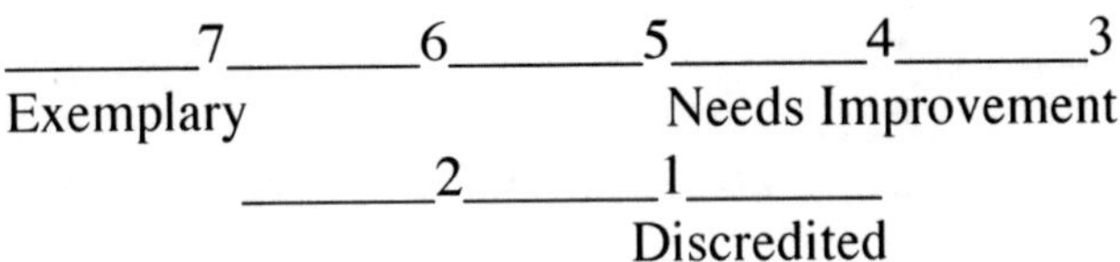
_______7_______6_______5_______4_______3
Exemplary Needs Improvement
_______2_______1_______
Discredited

d. Respectable: an orderly, disciplined, honorable man:

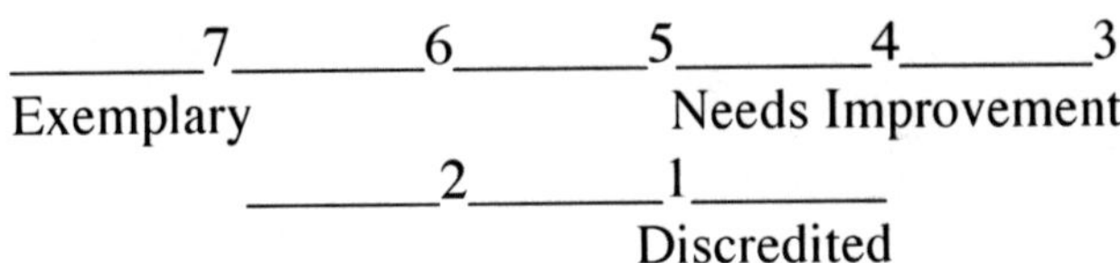
_______7_______6_______5_______4_______3
Exemplary Needs Improvement
_______2_______1_______
Discredited

e. Hospitable:

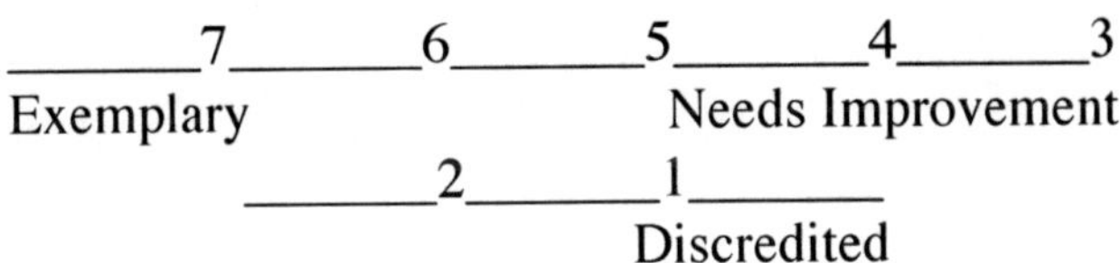
_______7_______6_______5_______4_______3
Exemplary Needs Improvement
_______2_______1_______
Discredited

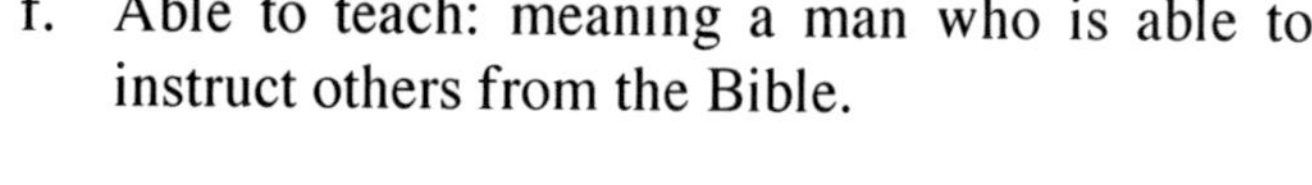

f. Able to teach: meaning a man who is able to instruct others from the Bible.

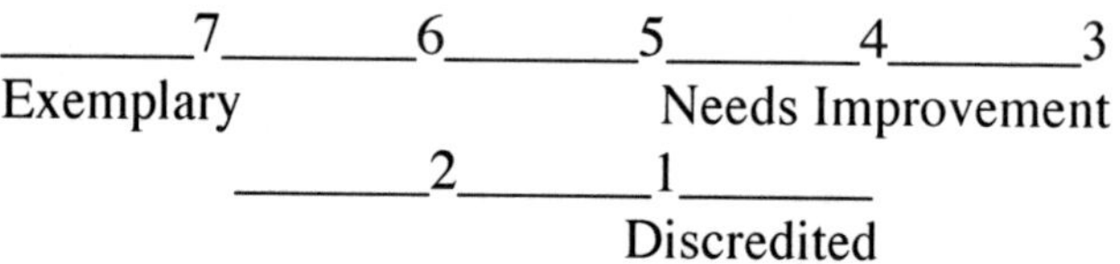

g. Not addicted to wine: a man whose habits and lifestyle do not damage his testimony.

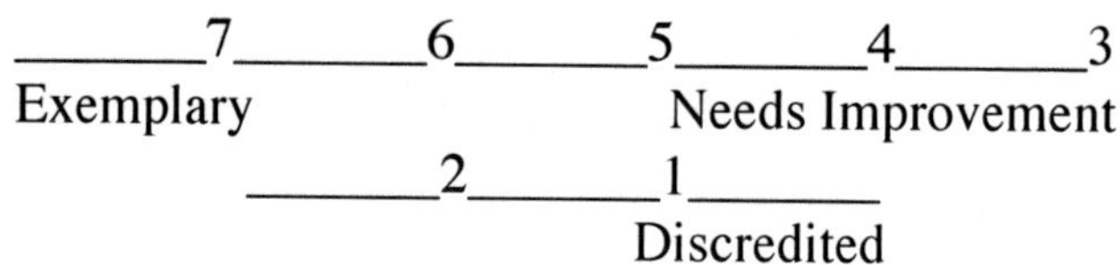

h. Not pugnacious: a man whose temper and emotions are in check.

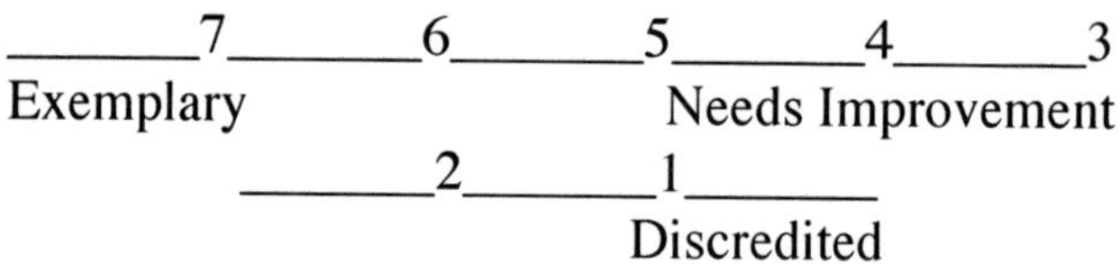

i. Gentle: a forbearing, gracious, conciliatory man.

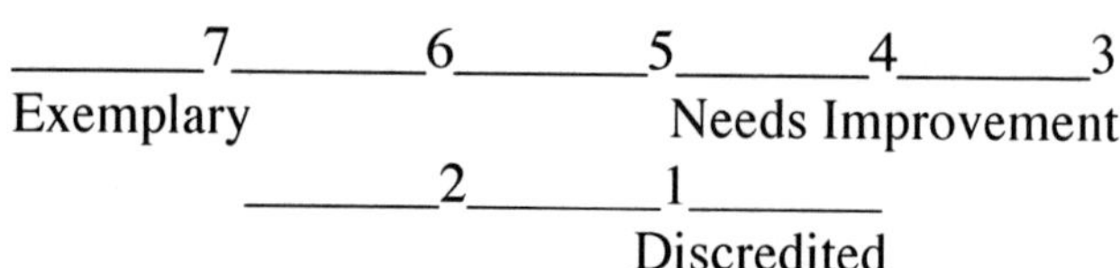

j. Peaceable: a non-contentious man, who is not quarrelsome:

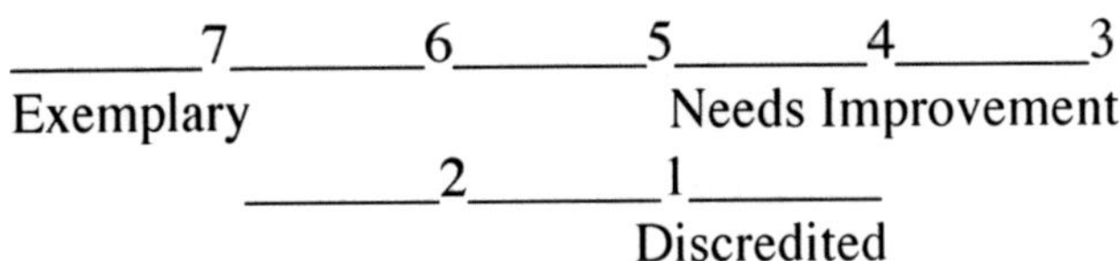

k. Free from the love of money: not materialistic and not in significant debt (bondage!)

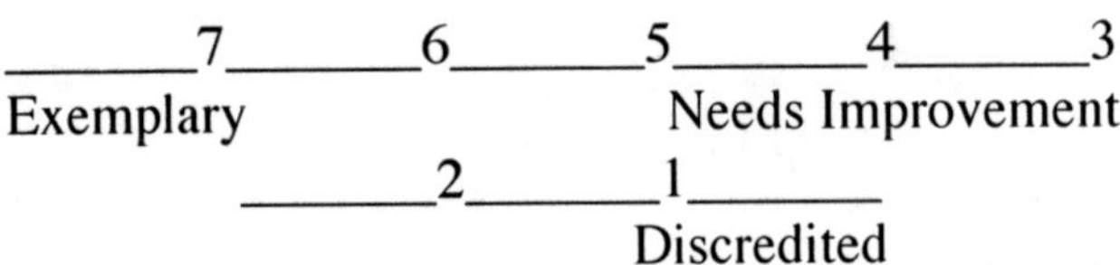

l. A man who manages his house well: a responsible Christian father, husband, and household manager.

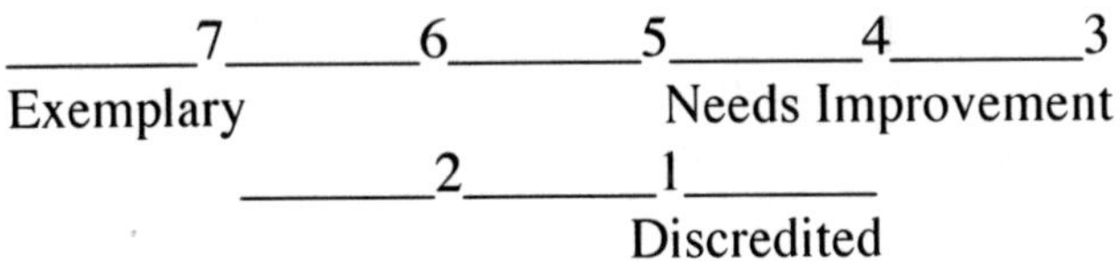

m. Not a new convert: a man who is spiritually mature, tested:

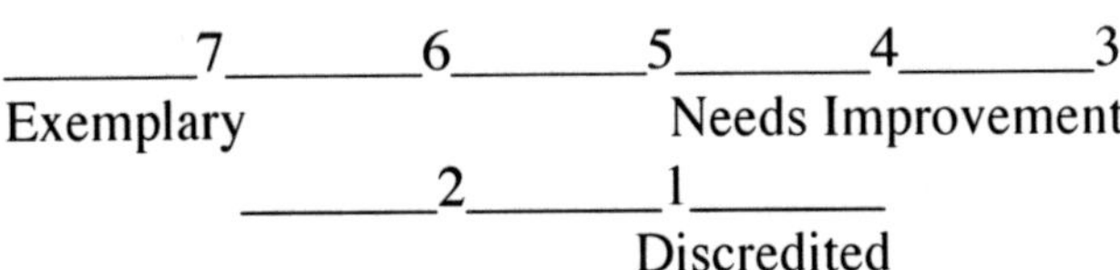

n. A man with a good reputation outside the Christian community:

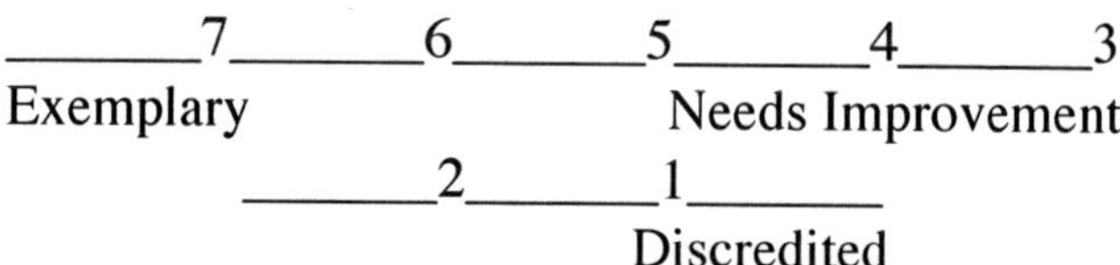

19. What else did you learn from the reading this time that you would like to comment on or ask about?

As you can see from these questions, we got 'up close and personal' really fast! From talking about our "fatal flaw," to how we work with groups or teams, to how well we believe we fit the qualifications for elder, as they are described by the Apostle Paul. I reminded the men all along the way that the goal is clear: we are looking for God to raise up the men He desires to serve this new church as elders. I believe it to be true: better not to have any elders at all than to have the wrong ones. If you lay hands on a man too quickly, before he has proven himself to be ready to serve as an elder, you are asking for nothing but trouble. I would prefer to see a new church plant start without any elders in place than to hastily appoint two or three men because we believe the church must have a plurality of elders. Isn't it true that there was already a church in Crete when Paul left Titus there? I believe it is. Did the churches that Paul and Barnabus planted on their missionary journey begin with elders in place? I don't think so. Remember the verse in Acts 14:23, where we are told Paul and Barnabus appointed elders in every church? These were churches in Lystra, Iconium and Antioch, cities the two great missionaries were *returning* to; the churches were already going strong there, presumably, and now there were men who were ready to serve as elders.

Don't misunderstand. I believe the ideal is to start with elders in place. But the pioneer works of the first great missionary team started from the ground up, with every member of the churches being brand-new converts! Most of our churches will not start that way, though we certainly pray and believe that God will use the new church to reach the lost.

I believe there are three primary considerations to make in choosing elders, whether you are choosing them for an existing church or for a new church plant. The first consideration is the presence of desire. Paul started his list of qualifications for elder with this: ***If a man desires the position of (an elder), he desires a good work.*** The two words translated "desire" in that verse are two different Greek words. The first means to reach out for, as if to desire something and take the necessary step to obtain it. The second word translated desire means, "to long for, to have your affections directed toward something." (Spiros Zhodiates, *The Complete Word Study New Testament*). I like the combination Paul used there because it indicates that there is something in the man's heart that is motivating him to action. He wants something, in a good way, and he wants it enough to change the status quo of his life to obtain it. All of my brothers out there reading this chapter know that one of our common flaws as men is that we believe this myth: "If I know something is true, that must mean I am *doing* it!" No, sorry, that's just not going to fly. Go ahead and check your bags on Reality Airlines and follow through on what you know is right. That's what an elder candidate needs: follow through. He has the desire to be an elder and he is willing to acknowledge that the desire came from God and that he needs to follow through, at least until the next step.

The next step is the second consideration to make in choosing an elder: he must be biblically qualified. There is no better place than 1 Timothy 3 or Titus 1 for the list of qualifications a potential church elder must meet. You know what I love about this list? It has nothing to do with social status. It has nothing to do with college degrees. It has nothing to do with ancestry. It has nothing to do with racial heritage or corporate success or business acumen or good looks or even spiritual gifts! The list of qualifications for elders focuses on character. It focuses on integrity. It focuses on spiritual maturity. Paul starts with "A bishop must then be blameless," and that fairly well says it all. He is not saying that an elder is perfect; that would make for a very short candidate list from your new church plant. There would be exactly zero men on it! He is also not referring to the man's life *before* salvation. We are new creations in Christ. (2 Cor. 5:17) No, by "blameless" Paul means "one who has nothing which an adversary could seize on" in order to make a charge. (Zhodiates) In other words, he is a man of integrity. He could run for President and not be brought down on moral charges. Blameless. Paul then goes on to describe how "blameless" looks when it is applied to a man's marriage, his temper, his hospitality, his habits, his money, and more. In each case, the man who is ready to serve as an elder is not perfect, but neither is he reproachable. His "progress," not his perfection, is evident to all.

An elder is required also to be able to teach. This is really the only measurement of his life that has anything to do with "ability." He may not have an especially strong gift of teaching or preaching. But he is able to teach. This would imply to me that he knows the Word and loves it. He is able to "rightly divide" the Word and can explain the truths of Scripture to any who ask.

He must also be a good manager of his home. Some would classify this as "ability," like teaching is an ability. I disagree. I believe the requirement that an elder be a man who "rules his house well, having his children in submission with all reverence" is a measure of his character, his integrity. In other words, does this man have a walk with the Lord that is the same at home as it is in the community and in the church? Does his walk match his talk when it comes to how he loves his wife and trains up his children? Is he obedient to the Lord in this crucial area of marriage and family? If not, then he is not ready to be an elder. As I have already said, "If it's not working at home, don't export it!" Paul says it very clearly: ***If a man does not know how to rule his own house, how will he take care of the church of God?*** (1 Timothy 3:5)

There is a third consideration, in my opinion. The man who is being examined to see if he is 'elder material' may have the desire. He may have the qualifications. But does he also have the time? Now, maybe this wasn't a problem in the first century. Maybe Paul never had to ask a brother if it was the right 'time' in his life to become an elder. But we must ask that today. If a man who is spiritually qualified and eager to become an elder just started a new business that is requiring his attention for 60 hours a week, I don't think he will be effective as an elder. There may be other extenuating circumstances that would give you pause before laying hands on a brother. By all means, ask the question and make sure you are getting an honest answer: Do you have time to be an elder? I think Strauch does an excellent job in his book making the case for how physically, emotionally, and spiritually demanding the elder's job is. If a man is going to 'do it right,' it will require much of him. Paul said to the Ephesian elders, "Therefore take heed to yourselves and to all the flock, among which the Holy Spirit has made you overseers, to shepherd the church of God which He purchased with His own blood." (Acts 20:28) If that doesn't send chills down your spine, you who are considering the work of an elder, then maybe you should re-consider. The church was purchased by the precious blood of Jesus, and we who are called by the Holy Spirit to shepherd must not take that lightly.

I meet with the other elders at Antioch every Sunday at 7:30am, in my office. We begin with prayer, usually praying for 10 minutes or so about the various needs in the church. Sometimes we pray longer, depending on how many concerns or needs there are. We then spend an hour or more talking about the church, what's going on, who's coming and going, what God is doing on all the various fronts of ministry. We may discuss the home groups and the shepherds who lead each group. We may talk about a mission trip that is coming up. We may talk about a problem we are facing in the church or a challenge we see in the community that we can address. Sometimes we will meet with someone in the congregation who needs to get our counsel. Sometimes we will meet with a missionary who is asking for our support. Once a month (the first Sunday), we meet together with the deacons and address any concerns or ideas they have to share. On the third Sunday of the month we meet at 7:00am with the shepherds (men who lead our home groups) and give them encouragement and hear reports from their home groups. After that we meet with all the men and young men of the church (ages 12 and up) for a Men's Breakfast. So, the elders meet together every Sunday, but on two of the four Sundays we are meeting also with larger circles of men in the church.

All of that is to say, if a man feels so pressured at work and at home that he would consider it a chore to come to church early every Sunday morning, he is probably too busy to be an elder. He may have the desire and he may be perfectly qualified...but it is simply not the right time. This is a great time for the elders to be able to speak into this brother's life and encourage him. If it is possible for him to free up his schedule in order to serve as an elder, we want him to do that if it is his desire. Sometimes this has been a red flag to show us that right now his priorities are out of order and he needs to work hard at restoring them to where they need to be. At other times this has been a perfect indicator that the

Lord has the man exactly where He wants him and that in the right time, when that time comes, the Lord will change the circumstances and bring freedom to serve as an elder. But not right now. This is a freeing thing, not just for the man and his family but for the elders as well! It is also a wonderful protection for the church body.

Chapter Five

Make an Appointment!

So when they had appointed elders in every church, and prayed with fasting, they commended them to the Lord in whom they had believed. (Acts 14:23)

The next step in the process is to appoint the elders whom God has clearly raised up. After the training period, the current elders should be able to see which of the men in the 'class' are qualified and ready. The elders at Antioch will ask these men individually to come and meet with us. In the elders' meeting, we will ask the man who is being considered for elder a number of questions. First, do you still have the desire to be an elder? Do you believe you are biblically qualified, based on the requirements of 1 Timothy 3, Titus 1 and 1 Peter 5? Does your wife have peace about you serving as an elder? Is there anything in your marriage or with your children that would hinder you from being an effective elder, with integrity?

Then we get into some *very* personal areas. Do you now or have you ever used pornography of any kind? It is rare to find a man today who has not been affected by pornography, and we are not eliminating men who were involved in it in their "BC" days. But if the man has been involved with porn since he became a committed disciple of Jesus Christ, and especially in the last few years, it is too soon to give him spiritual authority. There needs to be some distance between him and that sin. Our next question is, do you have any debt besides your mortgage? Again, we are not going to eliminate a man who has a car loan or a small amount of unsecured credit card debt. But if a man is drowning in debt and has trouble even making the minimum payments on his loans, can he effectively lead a church? We would counsel him to hit those debts with a vengeance and get them paid off or significantly paid down so that when he is appointed as an elder he can serve without distraction. *And* so that he will be able to counsel others in the body who have financial struggles. We will also ask the brother if he gives faithfully to the church. We believe the tithe is not a "have to" but a "get to" and that it is a minimum. We are certainly free to give much more than ten percent! But if a brother is not giving to the church, or giving very little, that is an indicator to us that there is a problem with stewardship. There is a problem with trusting God, perhaps. There may be an issue with transferring ownership of everything we have to God who is the owner! The next question we ask is this: Do you love the church and have a deep desire to see the church fed, led, cared for and protected? Finally, we ask the potential elder: Is there anything else that we have not asked you that would possibly surprise us if we knew about it?

After we have gone through these questions, and we have established that these men have a desire to serve, are qualified to serve, and have the time to serve, we take the next step: we ask the church to pray for these men and to consider them as potential elders. "If you have a question about any of these men, or if you have a concern about any of these men," we say to the entire congregation, "please come and talk to one of the current elders about it." This is done for two reasons.

First, these men we are praying about appointing to eldership are supposed to be "blameless," remember? "Above reproach." What if someone in the congregation has filed away an incident about one of these men, something that happened that would cause them to question his being qualified to serve as a shepherd? Wouldn't the elders of the church want to know about it before that brother is appointed? If someone comes forward with a question or a concern, we thank them for coming and we assure them that what they are doing is the right thing, even if their concern turns out to be minor. We ask them to share their concern with us and we listen, asking follow-up questions as necessary. Then we thank them and pray and they are free to go. The elders will then discuss the concern and debate its validity. If we believe, after prayer and discussion (usually over a period of a few weeks) that the concern is minor and something we can overlook, one of us will speak to the person who brought the concern to us and explain why we believe it is not something we need to explore further. If we believe that the concern has enough merit that we need to at least bring it to the potential elder's attention, we will ask him to meet with us for that purpose. How he responds to the meeting is an important matter. If we share the concern and the potential elder gets defensive or angry about it, though it is true and he admits that he 'did it,' then that may raise a red flag for us. Even if it is not true, how the brother reacts may be an indication of a problem with anger or defensiveness. He may not be quite as ready to serve as we thought he was. On the other hand, if we share the concern (anonymously, of course) and he responds with grace and humility, even though the concern itself is not a deal-breaker for us, then that will probably confirm to us that this is a man whom God has appointed. Of course, we also may hear a concern about a man that, if true, would mean a disqualification for him. This has not happened in our 20-year history as a church, and probably because we have the type of fellowship where the men are known to one another and the men who would be considered for elder are walking in integrity before the congregation.

The second reason we ask the congregation to pray about potential elders is simply that we want them to join us in the process. Though we are not a congregational-led church, and we never vote on any decisions, that does not mean that we don't value the input and the wisdom and the counsel we can receive from the members. They, too, have the Holy Spirit! We ask them to pray because we love them and we put a high premium on their involvement in the process. We want them to trust the leaders whom they will be following, and so it is common sense to us that we would ask them to pray with us about these men. I have had the pleasure many times to have someone come up to me after I have announced a name we are considering for elder and say, "Oh, I think he is a wonderful man of God, and I have often wondered why he wasn't an elder already! Good choice!" When you hear comments like that from the people who love *you* and follow your leadership, it is a blessing and an encouragement.

Once the congregation has had some time to consider the slate of potential elders (and we usually give them at least 30 days), we can proceed. We will meet with the men one last time in our weekly elders' meeting and ask if they still believe God is calling them to serve. They have been praying with their wives during this thirty-day period as well, and will often come into this final meeting fired-up and ready to go.

On that same Sunday, or one very soon, we will ask the elder-appointees to come down front at the end of the service. One of the current elders will read from 1 Timothy 3 or Titus 1 and make some comments about the importance of these biblical qualifications. We will announce to the congregation that these men have been taken through the training process and have been found ready and qualified to serve the flock as elders. We will give a charge to the elder-appointees that they are taking up a crucial responsibility to lead, feed, protect and care for the flock of God that was purchased with the precious blood of Christ. We also will give a charge to the congregation and remind them that these men will become elders and by virtue of that office should be respected and esteemed. We may read to them 1 Thessalonians 5:12-13: ***And we urge you, brethren, to recognize those who labor among you, and are over you in the Lord and admonish you, and to esteem them very highly in love for their work's sake. Be at peace among yourselves.*** The appointment of elders brings to the flock a responsibility to follow, just as it brings to the new elders a responsibility to lead! We may also read from Hebrews 13:7, ***Remember those who rule over you, who have spoken the word of God to you, whose faith follow, considering the outcome of their conduct.*** And also verse 17: ***Obey those who rule over you, and be submissive, for they watch out for your souls, as those who must give account. Let them do so with joy and not with grief, for that would be unprofitable for you.*** Following this, the men will kneel and the elders will lay hands on and pray for them

Why would we read these verses to the congregation? Because we want to push this in their faces and remind them of their slavish duty to obey? Not at all! We would read these verses because we live in a wicked and perverse culture that is increasingly casting off all restraint with regard to authority. There is little or no respect for authority in the home, in the schools, in the workplace, and even in the churches of our land. Those who would be a part of a healthy church plant, heed this: you cannot have a healthy, biblical church unless the people are taught very clearly from the Word what it means for them to follow the leadership God has raised up. You also cannot have a healthy, biblical church unless the men who *are* leading have the biblical qualifications elders must have and see that their responsibility is to lead, not to lash; to feed, not to fleece; to love, not to lord over!

The question inevitably comes up when I talk with people about elders, "How long do they serve?" I realize that in our corporate-minded world, we often think in terms of job appointments that only last a few years or even a few months. I am not opposed to the idea of a man serving a three-year term and then rotating off the elder board. But that idea, to me, smacks of a corporate model and I honestly cannot find precedent for it in Scripture. Can you imagine Peter telling the church in Jerusalem, after serving his three-year rotation: "I am tired of helping to take care of this church. Frankly, I am weary of dealing in sheep-dung. I am going fishing!" Somehow I get the idea that Peter was involved integrally in leadership in the church until the day that he was literally not able to do it any longer because he was hanging upside down on a cross! At Antioch, our elders serve as long as they can. We have never had an elder step down because of personal moral failure. We *have* had a couple of occasions where an elder has stepped down because one of his children was struggling with some sin issues and needed his intentional leadership at home.

Another question that comes up with regularity is, "How soon after a man joins the church can we make him an elder?" This is a great question because, to be honest, we live in a celebrity-crazy culture. What happens if someone who is popular or powerful starts coming to our church? Even though that person is a new believer, we may want to go ahead and give him some responsibility, even ask him to serve as an elder or come on staff! After all, this is Mr. So-n-So, and he is the CEO of a multi-million dollar enterprise. He has 360 employees who stand ready to do whatever he wants, whenever he wants it, and he is a force to be reckoned with in our society! Don't you think it would turn the community upside down if we made him chairman of the board or head elder or something?

Well, at the risk of offending, pardon me while I get sick to my stomach. I have one question for you, should you jettison all caution and take Mr. Big Shot and make him an elder: What will you do with Paul's qualification that an elder is "Not a novice, lest being puffed up with pride he fall into the same condemnation as the devil"? (1 Timothy 3:6) There is never a good reason to make a new believer an elder. Even in a new church plant. If the only men in the new church plant are new converts, then you have to wait! If you lay hands on a man who has no spiritual maturity but is a babe drinking milk, you are courting disaster, as Paul makes plain in this warning.

But let me take it even further. Paul's word for "novice" means literally, "newly planted." Now I know that the common understanding of that interpretation means "newly converted," however I would suggest that Paul may have also meant, "newly joined." I could be wrong, but I think there is a danger in making a man an elder who, though mature and biblically qualified, is new to the flock. To make a point, I would even suggest that if Franklin Graham or John Piper moved into your community and started attending your church, you would be foolish to make either one of them an elder the next week. Or month. What?! Are not Franklin Graham and John Piper absolute paragons of Christian maturity? Oh, yes. I would sit at their feet and learn from either one of them. They each have more maturity than I. But in this case, they would need to wait to become elders, because elders are shepherds who lead real, live people, and you know as well as I do that the people of any church want and need to be led by elders they know, love and trust. I don't know Mr. Graham or Mr. Piper and it would take a while before I would feel comfortable following their lead as my elders. In our experience at Antioch, we have never asked someone to be an elder until he has been a member of the church for at least a year. There may come a time when we will make an exception to that "rule," but I cannot imagine what circumstances would require us to do so.

Another question that comes up frequently with regard to elders is this one: "What's the difference between an elder and a pastor?" Well, on the one hand, there is no difference among them at all. The Bible speaks of two offices in the church, the office of elder and the office of deacon. There is not an office of 'pastor.' At Antioch, there are four elders and we have equal authority. Each of us is charged with the responsibility to shepherd the flock, to lead, feed, protect and care for the church. In one sense, then, we are all pastors, bishops, overseers, elders. However, and this is where I would differ with Alexander Strauch, one of us at Antioch *is* called 'pastor.' It is not an office but a ministry. Strauch writes, "To call one elder 'pastor' and the rest 'elders'…is to act without biblical precedence. To do so will not result in a biblical eldership." What Strauch is concerned with there is legitimate: raising one man up above the rest will result in a hierarchical leadership. I agree. That is why we do not do that. The pastor at Antioch is not any more important than any other saint there. The pastor at Antioch is one of the elders, but he is the "first among equals," to use a term that Strauch uses in *Biblical Eldership*. My job as pastor of Antioch is to be out front as the point man, if you will, to help lead the leaders. When we meet together every Sunday morning, the others look to me for leadership in that meeting. When we have to decide on an issue, however, I have just one "vote." We all agree on major decisions or we do not *make* a decision. I cannot make unilateral decisions regarding anything of significance in the church. This is a safeguard for me, because I am under the authority of the elders, just as any elder is. This is also a safeguard for the church, because there are three other men who will help make sure the church is not led by a man who has no accountability. As the old saying goes, "power corrupts, and absolute power corrupts absolutely."

What happens when I die, or the Lord decides to move me to another place? I believe the church will not miss a beat but go right on advancing the Kingdom of God in the same way it is now. Where will the next 'pastor' come from, the next "first among equals?" Our prayer is that he will come from Antioch. Think about it. If we believe that an elder should not be a novice, and that word can mean newly planted, or new to the fellowship, then how could we hire someone from the outside to become the pastor? We couldn't. By God's grace, we won't. That means that we had better be about the job of training up future leadership. That means that we should give the current elders and other spiritually mature men in the church opportunities to preach, to lead, to make decisions, to do the work of ministry. Someone said once, "Don't just delegate responsibility; delegate authority." Amen! I believe this with all my heart: the fruit of a ministry where authority is delegated is a healthy crop of leaders who are thriving in their own right.

Let me offer one final word about elders and how they lead. There is a vital difference between consensus leadership and unanimity leadership. In the latter, no decision can be made unless every single elder is in total agreement and is ready to move forward. With consensus leadership, each elder is free to say to the others, "Though that is not the ideal decision to make in this case, in my opinion, I will not stand in the way of you making that decision." In other words, he is willing to consent, even though he is not really excited about or motivated by the decision. This has happened many times over the years at Antioch. An example might be when a particular missionary or mission organization asks our church for a large donation, perhaps to help build a church building or dig some clean wells or provide a new used-car for the national pastor at the mission. It might happen that one of the elders is not in favor of spending the money in that way, but the other elders think it's a good idea. The elder with the reservation will usually yield, unless he believes we would be making a mistake to send the money. He would say something like, "Though I am not convinced this is the best decision we could make, I am not convinced it is the wrong decision, either. I am willing to go along with the majority." Consensus leadership prevents stalemates, but there is always the option for any of the elders to stop a decision from going forward if he feels strongly that it would be a mistake.

One of the elders of Antioch's most recent church plant read the paragraph above and wrote to me with this suggestion:

> The elder who shows less excitement for a decision, but who is not willing to oppose it, should still support the decision enthusiastically once the decision is made. He should especially avoid the temptation to disown the decision if it goes bad, sowing seeds of division among the elders, or among the flock.

Amen! This is an important point that speaks to the spirit of good leadership and goes beyond just the 'mechanics.'

Before we turn our attention to the people who will join your family-integrated church, let me state that the issue of leadership cannot be over-emphasized. I am of the opinion that the church simply will not rise above the level of its leadership. The church that is led by godly men who love the Lord and are devoted to His Word and to the equipping of the saints for the work of ministry—that church will thrive and be a city on a hill. The church that is led by carnal men who are in positions for which they are not qualified—that church will languish and stumble and stagger and, most likely, collapse. And as Jesus said of the man who built his house on the sand, when the collapse came, "the ruin of that house was great." May it never be said of the church you are praying and preparing to plant, brothers!

Chapter Six

Come and Join Us!

Hey, do you know why fire trucks are red? Well, fire trucks have four wheels and eight men; everybody knows that four plus eight is twelve. There are twelve inches in a foot, and a foot is a ruler. Queen Elizabeth II was a ruler, and also the name of one of the largest ships on the seven seas. Seas have fish and fish have fins. Finns fought the Russians. Russians used to be called "Reds." Fire trucks are always "rushin'." Therefore, fire trucks are red.

If you think that sounds bizarre, you should hear the reasons people give for not joining a church!

We have talked about the foundational principle of finding and training good elders. Let's talk about helping the people who come to the church get settled in as members. "But," you may say, "I don't believe in church membership. I believe it is unbiblical to ask people to join the church!" Some may say they don't join a church because there is a good chance they will be moving in the next five or ten years. Still others won't join because they had a bad experience at their last church. Some won't join because they would be "embarrassed" to have to stand up front and let the elders introduce them to the congregation. Others don't join because they would never join anything that would accept them as a member. Oops, sorry on that last one. A little bit of lame humor.

Why join a church? Very simply, because I believe it is the biblical thing to do. Consider the following passage from John Piper's book, *When I Don't Desire God.*

Just as God ordained that there be teachers, living and dead, so he ordained that the whole Body of Christ speak the Word of God to each other every day in the fight for joy. "Exhort one another every day." Specifically, "Let us consider how to stir up one another to love and good works, not neglecting to meet together, as is the habit of some, but encouraging one another, and all the more as you see the Day drawing near" (Heb. 10:24-25). All of us should feel the calling to exhort others with the Word of God. But that's not my point here. My point here is that you should make sure this is done to you. Put yourself in some kind of fellowship, small enough so that this one-another ministry is happening. One of my first questions in dealing with a joyless saint is, "Are you in a small group of believers who care for each other and pray for each other and 'consider how to stir one another up to love'"? Usually the answer is no.

THE WORD OF GOD IS A COMMUNITY TREASURE

As much as I stress Bible reading, and Bible memorization, and Bible meditation, and reading great books on Bible doctrine, all of that could sound very individualistic. It suits my American bent. But the Word of God is meant to be a community treasure and a community event. It should be alive in the fellowship of believers. This is probably the normal form that the gift of prophecy should take today: anointed, Spirit-guided speaking and application of Scripture in timely ways for each person's need. That is what we need from each other in the fight for joy. Don't rest until you have sought out, or called together, a group of believers where this is happening.

Let me be very specific in regard to church membership in the fight for joy. I know it is possible to be a member of a church—that is, to have your name on an official roll—and not be connected to other believers in a way that stirs up spiritual life and joy and obedience. Indeed it is possible to be a member of a local church and not even be a believer. Nevertheless I believe it is the will of Christ for all of his people to be responsible members of Christ-exalting, Bible-believing local churches. This may be impossible in some locations. God knows that and will supply what we need if the normal means of grace are lacking. But in ordinary circumstances Christians should be responsible members of a local church.

When the New Testament uses the word member to refer to a Christian in relation to a local body of believers, it uses the word first metaphorically. That is, we are members of a local body of believers the way hands and feet are members of the human body. "As the body is one and has many members, and all the members of the body, though many, are one body, so it is with Christ. . . . If the foot should say, 'Because I am not a hand, I do not belong to the body,' that would not make it any less a part of the body" (1 Cor. 12:12, 15). This is a picture not of the universal body of Christ, but of the local expression of that body in a specific place. We know this for several reasons.

One reason is that when Paul refers to the universal body of Christ, he says the "head" is Christ himself. "He is the head of the body, the church" (Col. 1:18; 2:19; Eph. 5:23). But when Paul refers to the local body of believers, he uses the term "head" as just another member, like hand or foot: "The eye cannot say to the hand, 'I have no need of you,' nor again the head to the feet, 'I have no need of you'" (1 Cor. 12:21). Another reason we know that the picture of "membership" in 1 Corinthians 12 is membership in a local body of believers, and not just membership in the universal body of Christ, is that it speaks of close relationships of care and responsibility that go with this membership: "God has so composed the body . . . that there may be no division in the body, but that the members may have the same care for one another" (1 Cor. 12:24-25). This kind of mutual care is not possible in the universal body of Christ, but only in local expressions of that body.

Therefore, it is clear that the apostle Paul moves beyond the metaphorical use of member (hand and foot and head and eye) to the real, personal, responsible membership in a local church. Membership moves from the metaphorical connectedness to real, concrete organizational connectedness that creates the expectation of both care and accountability. This is why Paul can take church discipline so seriously and even speak of the rare cases when a member is put out of the church. "For what have I to do with judging outsiders? Is it not those inside the church whom you are to judge? God judges those outside. 'Purge the evil person from among you'" (1 Cor. 5:12-13). Such a formal removal would not be possible if there were no formal membership.

I stress this biblical perspective on church membership because we live in a day when people shun responsibility and accountability. We are very individualistic and resistant to others holding us to any standard that might cross our immediate desires. But God loves us and does not call us to what is bad for us. Church membership is a gift of grace. Like all relationships (marriage, parenting, employment, teams, citizenship), it has its pain. But, more than most of us realize, it has its life-sustaining, faith-strengthening, joy-preserving effect according to God's plan and mercy. The Christ-displaying, corporate ministry of the Word of God comes to us in church membership in ways that we cannot predict. I urge you not to cut yourself off from this blessing by staying on the edges of Christ's church. (pages 129-132)

I am indebted to John Piper for this clear word from THE Word. I would add to his biblical reasons for joining a church what Peter said when he exhorted elders to "Shepherd the flock which is among you." (1 Peter 5:2). Using the shepherd/sheep analogy, how would a shepherd know which sheep to tend if they were not his? A shepherd in New Zealand does not leave his house every morning and just go "take care of some random sheep." "How did your day go, dear?" "It was great! I found two sheep in the neighbor's pasture, lured them down to the stream, and took care of them all day. Now they belong to me!" No, that would be sheep rustling, which by the way happens a lot in our churches these days. The shepherd with integrity will know the sheep who are his, just as Jesus said in John 10. He will even call them by name and they will follow him. In the same way, the elders who lead must know who is following. They will know them by name because these "sheep" have come and indentified themselves with this particular "flock." Some might argue that you can do that without officially "joining" the church, but I would respond that you can also have a civil union, recognized by the laws of the state, with a woman you have lived with for a number of years. But it is not the same as making a commitment, taking a vow, promising your faithfulness before God and witnesses!

One final argument I would make for church membership has to do with being under the protective authority of the leadership in a church. When a family or single stands down front at Antioch and states their intention to join the church that day, having gone through the New Members' class and having prayed and heard from the Lord that this is the church He wants them to commit to, they are announcing that to the elders. They are announcing that to the congregation, their brothers and sisters they will be locking arms with in battle. They are *also* announcing that to the "principalities" and "powers" and the "rulers of the darkness of this age," the "spiritual hosts of wickedness in the heavenly places." (Ephesians 6:12). Now don't get me wrong. We don't spend any time talking to demons, nor should we! But we do wage war against them. Our war is not with flesh and blood. Our enemy is a ruler and he has an army, if you will, and a strategy and a battle plan. When a believer announces before God and His people that he is standing under the authority and the covering of a local fellowship and her elders, I believe hell trembles. That family or that single person is announcing that he is not a lone ranger, he is not an isolated individual just trying to serve "my Jesus." He is announcing that he is taking up arms under the Captain of the Lord of Hosts, and under the elders the Lord has raised up in this particular local fellowship. That is an important step for believers to take, dear reader. It is not just foolish for a believer to get so disgusted with church that he decides to "chuck it all" and go home. It is deadly. It is not just a bad idea for a family to wander from pillar to post for months and sometimes years, searching for the church that will be just right for their family. It is dangerous. How many of us can name at least one family who has become disillusioned or disappointed with church and has decided just to have church at home as a family? This is not just a shame, it is unbiblical. The Bible knows nothing of a family or a single person having "church" without being vitally and integrally connected to others of the faith. By the way, I like the truth that is found in this statement, as we consider those who have been disillusioned with the church: "You cannot become disillusioned unless you first had an illusion." In many cases, that disgruntled church member who chucks it all went into the church from the very beginning with an illusion. The bubble was burst and he shook the dust off his garments and stomped out, feeling very justified in leaving. That is just the beginning of his troubles.

Is there a perfect church? No, never was, never will be. Read Acts 5-6 and find out how the bloom came off the rose in Jerusalem. The elders of the church who had *experienced Pentecost* had to deal with problems in the church! But here is what I love about that church and what I believe every church should strive to emulate: when the problems arose, the leadership dealt with them in a way that was biblical and Christ-honoring. As a result of that, the church grew in numbers and in maturity. The people did not leave because there were problems in the church. They stayed and many more joined them. I hear some of you saying right now, "Yeah, but the problem in the church in Jerusalem was not with the leadership." You are exactly right, and I understand that there is so much hurt and confusion and sin that can result when leaders fall. But God is able to redeem. He is ready to spare that precious fellowship and make it stronger, *if* the other leaders will step up and do their jobs and *if* the rest of the fellowship will pray and follow. At the same time, listen to this warning to pastors and elders, from Matt Schmucker of Capitol Hill Baptist Church (and 9Marks Ministry) as he blogged about Governor Eliot Spitzer's resignation amidst a scandal:

As dead flies give perfume a bad smell, so a little folly outweighs wisdom and honor." Ecclesiastes 10:1

This verse came to mind when I heard the announcement of NY governor Eliot Spitzer's resignation upon revelation of his adulterous activity. I don't mean to suggest that his behavior equaled "a little folly." Nor do I mean to suggest all his "legal" activity as attorney general and governor was above reproach; I have no comment on those issues.

I'm simply saying to all of you pastors, elders, deacons and seminarians that it doesn't take much folly — just a little — to wipe out years of otherwise faithful service. Folly is weightier, it seems, than wisdom and honor. We're called to avoid even a little of it.

How many pastors have been wiped out and sidelined from the gospel fight because of a little folly? I pray that this rising generation of men would be different. Flee, brothers, flee from folly!

Psalm 119:1 says, "Blessed are they whose ways are blameless, who walk according to the law of the Lord."

Amen. May God give us grace and wisdom and keep us from even a hint of folly that would bring down our ministry and bring shame to His name!

Now, let's consider this matter of church membership. Here is what we do at Antioch.

I will encourage a new family to visit at least for a month or so before they go through the new members' class. Usually they will take my advice and extend it for 2-3 months. ☺ That is fine but I encourage visitors not to "date the church," as Josh Harris calls it, but get to the place very quickly where they can make a commitment.

The new members' class meets either two or three times, depending upon the need. If there are a lot of families going through it at the same time, then it may take three sessions. If there is just a handful, we can usually get through the material in two sessions. We will meet after church on Sundays, and try to get started by 12:15pm. I encourage the families to bring a lunch if they would like, and we meet in one of the classrooms around several tables that are put together. They are welcome to bring their children to the class, and especially older children are encouraged to come and listen.

Sometimes one of the older siblings will take their younger brothers and sisters outside to play or to the nursery. But the parents have the option of keeping everybody in (remember, this is a *family-integrated* church!).

The first class will begin with prayer, followed by introductions around the table. I ask each man to introduce himself, his wife and his children, to share how they came to know the Lord Jesus, and then how they found out about our church. Depending on the size of the group, this can take a while, but you do not want to rush it or skip it, for two reasons. First, no one should be allowed to join a church until they are members of THE church! If they do not have a clear testimony of a relationship with Jesus Christ, then you have a wonderful opportunity. The fact that they want to join your fellowship is a clear indication that the Lord is working in their hearts, in my opinion. So, you would want to either pull them aside after the class to talk about salvation, or make an appointment to get together at another time, very *soon*. The second reason not to skip the introductions and testimonies is that this may be the first real introduction this family or single has had to you, the pastor or one of the elders. If it is clear from the leader's demeanor that he really just wants to get through his material and doesn't have time to have a "chat" with the people who are visiting the church, that will be a warning flag for many. I don't know about you, but I would want to know from the very outset that the church I am considering putting my family into is led by men who love the Lord, His Word, *and* His people!

After the introductions, I will begin to give the history of our church. I have divided the New Members' class into three sections, labeled simply, "Where We Came From," "Who We Are," and "Where We are Going." In this first section, I will go over a brief history of how Antioch started, why we chose the name (more about names in a later chapter), and how God changed us from a program-driven church to a family-integrated church. Most of the time, the people have read my first book, *Family-Integrated Church*, and they know the history of Antioch. But I will go over the main points of our development anyway, and then open the floor for discussion and questions. I encourage you to make it clear all the way through the class that you welcome and invite any and all questions. In my experience, the very occasional challenge to your authority is worth the freedom that opening yourself to honest discussion will bring to the class. When the discussion time is over, we close in prayer.

The second class will begin with prayer and a brief review of what we had talked about the previous week. Then I will begin to share three main points with the class as they relate to "Who We Are." In this 60-90 minute time period, I want to first share about the doctrine of our church. What do we believe is essential doctrine? What do we believe is non-essential and we would not break fellowship over if there is disagreement? I like the motto of the reformers: *In essentials, unity; in non-essentials, liberty; in all things, charity.* It is during this time that I share the non-negotiables with the prospective members and tell them quite candidly that if they do not agree with all of these, they are in the wrong new members' class. These essentials of the faith were mentioned (and partly listed) in chapter 3.

Why is it important to draw a line in the sand, here? Because again, if you marry in haste, you will repent in leisure! If someone joins your church who really does not believe in the authority and the sufficiency of Scripture, you are asking for trouble. It is inevitable that trouble will arise, and probably very soon after they join the church! Sometimes people who are 'courting' a church will put on their best behavior and they will overlook anything in you or the church that they don't like. Then as soon as they say "I do," they take off the kid gloves and put on the brass knuckles, and it is *on*! It is much better to make every attempt in the 'courting stage' with prospective members to find out if they are in agreement with your vision and philosophy of ministry. The new members' class will *help* to accomplish this goal, but only if the class members are totally honest with you and with themselves. Sometimes a person doesn't know how important something is to him until that something is no longer there. We have had people come to Antioch and fall in love with the church and become a member and get involved in the lives of the people. Then 2 or 3 years down the road, and sometimes longer, they realize that there is something missing. They overlooked it in the honeymoon stage and then when they realized it was a problem for them, they tried to continue to overlook it. They prayed about it, they may have talked to the pastor or one of the other elders about it, and they still can't shake it. It is at that point that there is a crisis of faith. They can either lay down that thing that has emerged in their soul as an "essential," or they can try to convince the leadership of the church that they (the elders) need to change the direction of the church to accommodate this person's conviction, or they can leave. I will use an example that has not happened at our church to illustrate this point. We take communion once a month at Antioch. Suppose Mr. & Mrs. Smith start coming to Antioch and really love it. They get involved in a home group, they are regulars on Sunday morning, they go through the new members class and join. All along they know that Antioch takes communion once a month. They have learned that through experience (in several months of attendance), and they have learned it through the new members class. Now suppose Mr.& Mrs. Smith moved here from another state, where they were involved in a church that took the Lord's Supper every week. They didn't know that weekly communion was as important to them as it is until they had been at Antioch for about 2 years. In those two years, they had taken communion 24 times instead of 104 times. They knew that was going to be the deal when they joined but at the time they were so impressed with the life of the church, the preaching, the worship, the ministry to the community, the missions emphasis, and more. They told themselves, "Taking communion every week is *not* an essential for us. We love it here and we are going to join. We believe with all our heart that God is leading us to join." They do, and now here they are, two years later, wondering if they really had heard from God back then. They agonize over it, they talk to their home group leaders, they even make an appointment to go and talk with the elders about it. But in the final analysis, when they realize that the church is going to continue on its present course, they decide they will have to leave. There are tears and a sad farewell, and the Smiths start their search for another church. They know it will be tough. They have already tested the waters a few times during this doubting stage, and they know that they can go to ABC Church just across town, where they take communion every Sunday. But they know the music there is not exactly what they prefer. The preaching there is OK, but tends to be a little on the dry side. They know they can also go to XYZ Church just down the street. They take communion there every Sunday, too, but there is a youth group, the worship style is a little over the top, and the preaching tends to be topical.

Some of you have been there. Not to XYZ Church, but to the place of frustration. You have looked and looked, and you cannot find all the pieces that you like in a church. Guess what? You never will. That's my guess, based on more than 21 years of experience as a pastor. There is no perfect church, not simply because every church is filled with sinners like you and me. There is no perfect church, period. No church, even the one you help to *start*, will have all and be all that you want. If it is, you probably are a control freak and though it may seem perfect to you, it will not be 'perfect' for anyone else. In fact, keep it up and you will be worshiping all by yourself one day!

What's the point? Simply this. We need to learn to lay down our preferences and allow the Lord to teach us to esteem others as better than ourselves. If something is an essential to you and you cannot substantiate it as an essential in the Bible, then I would suggest you be prepared to lay it on the altar. If the church you are in preaches sound doctrine, worships Jesus with all their heart, builds the family and equips the men to lead, then you are way ahead of the game, my friend.

The second New Members Class, then, is a very important one, as you have probably gathered. Establish what the essentials are, and then have an open discussion about the non-essentials. I will usually ask it several times during each class: *What are your questions? What do you want to know about what we believe? Are there any doctrinal distinctions that you are concerned about or want to ask about? Please feel free. There are no questions that are off-limits.* If they sense that I am being sincere, they will feel the freedom to ask questions.

The second point of emphasis I want to make during this second New Members' class has to do with our leadership. Our church's website was just revamped in April of 2007, and since then we have been able to keep up with the number of hits on each page of it. By far the most popular one is the Leadership page. That is where those who are interested can find out who the elders and the deacons are, what their families look like, what kind of jobs the men have, etc.

Why would that page get more hits than any of the others, even more than the page about what we believe or the calendar of upcoming events or the blogs? I don't know for sure, but my guess is that people who are looking for a church are very concerned about the leadership. It is true in the new members classes I teach every year. Everyone is interested in finding out how the church is governed, who the elders and deacons are, how they are selected, and sometimes, why we don't have congregational votes! I would be the same way. Nearly at the top of my list, were I to go on a church-search with my family, would be understanding who the leaders are and what kind of character they have, and what they believe about their roles and responsibilities.

So, I spend a good amount of time explaining the leadership model of the church. We talk about the Scriptures that support a church being led by a plurality of elders (Acts 14:23, 20:17-38; 1 Timothy 3, Titus 1, 1 Peter 5, etc). We discuss the roles and responsibilities of the elders and the deacons. And again, I ask them to ask any question they like. Sometimes church discipline will come up as a question. The answer is yes. Sometimes women elders will come up as a question. The answer is no. No matter the question, I try and answer it with what the Word of God says. It's the final answer, after all!

The third new members' class will discuss "Where We are Going." In this class, I will ask again if there are any questions that have been generated by our discussions in the first two classes. After a couple has meditated for a week on what we believe and how we are led, there are sometimes questions that arise. I want to give them every opportunity to ask those questions *before* they decide to join the church.

Next, we will discuss the vision of the church for planting other churches. Since that is what this book is all about, there is no need to explain it here, but I will say that church-planting, and all that goes with it, has always been a key component of who we are as a church, even in the years when we were not ready to do it. A young man of 14 years old has the necessary ingredients in him to be a father, but he is not mature enough yet to enter that arena. It is a good thing, though, if he already has a desire to have children one day! Church planting is in our bloodstream at Antioch, and those who come here will certainly be 'infected.' We want them to know that up front.

I will also share with them about our stewardship of the building we are using. It is a miracle how God provided for us, without debt, to be able to enter a lease-to-purchase agreement with the folks who owned our church building before. This is discussed in Chapter 17 ("God or Mammon?") of my book, *Family-Integrated Church.* Whenever I share the story with anyone, it encourages them in their walk by faith. Incidentally, can we not trust the Son of God, the One who said, "I will build My church," to provide for our facility needs *without* debt? I believe we can and we must.

Finally, I will go over what I consider the essential stewardship issues for a new member. Remember Paul said in 1 Corinthians 4:2, "Moreover it is required in stewards that one be found faithful." A steward is someone who manages property that belongs to someone else. He is accountable, then, to the property owner for how well he manages. It is the same with every believer. We are stewards of the mystery of the gospel, of spiritual gifts, of health and wealth and intellectual abilities and a host of other 'properties' which all belong to God. We will one day give an account to God for how we managed what He gave to us. I believe it is important for potential church members to know up front what is expected of them as stewards before they ever join. I have divided this into three large areas: stewardship of Ministry, Morals, and Money. Sorry if the use of alliteration turns you off, here. I don't normally use it in my sermons, but in this case, it fits without being forced.

Stewardship of Ministry

Every member of the body of Christ has two things, guaranteed. This is in addition to salvation, of course! Each member has a spiritual gift. Each member has 168 hours a week. Let's examine the first statement by looking at 1 Peter 4:10:

"As each one has received a gift, minister it to one another, as good stewards of the manifold grace of God."

How many who belong to Christ have received a gift? Each one. It is not dependent on ability, race, national origin, intellectual capacity, or anything else. Every single person born of the Spirit has received a gift. When did each person receive it? Already. Peter says it clearly, using a past tense verb, "has received."

Who gave each believer a spiritual gift? The Holy Spirit. Paul says it clearly, "But one and the same Spirit works all these things, distributing to each one individually as He wills." (1 Corinthians 12:11)

For what purpose did the Spirit give each believer a gift? Here's where it gets exciting. Back to 1 Peter 4:10, and Peter tells us the gift is given so that we might "minister it to one another." There is so much packed into that tiny phrase, but let me suggest just a few truths. First, the gift is a tool not a trophy. It is not given to be admired but to be used. Second, the gift is for others, not for the user. You could almost say that the gift really does not 'work' until you give it away. Third, the gift is to be used in the context of the church. There may be times when your spiritual gift intrigues a nonbeliever or piques the attention of a skeptic, but it is not given for that primary purpose. The gifts are given so that the church will grow up, be healthy, and give glory to God.

How many gifts are there? There is argument over this detail, but one thing is crystal clear. The gifts are plural not singular. Paul makes it clear in 1 Corinthians how ridiculous the body of Christ would be if we were all an eye or an ear. Peter says here that we are to be good stewards of the gifts as they represent "the manifold grace of God." The word, "manifold" literally means various, or even "many-colored." God gives grace and that grace takes many different forms. Part of being an effective member of the body of Christ is not only knowing what your gift is, but learning to appreciate the others as well. Without them we would be all the poorer.

What is the requirement, then, for every believer? Stewardship! Peter said "...minister it to one another as good stewards..." God does not throw a church together haphazardly but carefully, with purpose and with design. I always tell new families or singles who believe they are called to come and join our church that God has brought them here because we need them and they need us. The church will be more mature if they are here, loving, serving, worshiping, and using their gifts.

I will not spend much time on it here, but I encourage you to look at Romans 12 sometime and see what Paul has to say about spiritual gifts. It is interesting to note that there are only seven gifts mentioned in this book of "systematic theology," and some contend it is because every born again believer has been given one of those seven. He may have been given more gifts as well, but the one he has from that list in Romans 12 is his "motivational gift." In other words, it is like a pair of glasses that colors how he looks at the church and motivates him to help meet the needs there. A person with the motivational gift of mercy, for example, will mostly see people who are suffering in some way and will be moved to try and relieve that suffering. The "prophet" has a primary desire to promote truth and has a very low sin-tolerance. Each of the seven gifts is necessary for balance and maturity and the healthy church will have a good number of people with each gift.

Let's talk about the second 'gift' God has given to every believer, the gift of time. We all get 168 hours a week, guaranteed, so I encourage the potential members to be faithful in their stewardship of those hours. We have two very important gatherings each week at Antioch. One is Sunday morning, when the whole body gathers for worship and teaching. The second is mid-week (usually Wednesday), when the body gathers in different homes for fellowship, Bible Study, and prayer. We do have other meetings that are regularly scheduled, like the men's breakfast on the third Sunday morning of each month, but they are not "required," if you will. I encourage new members to make every effort to attend Sunday worship and mid-week home groups faithfully. I may even say, "Even when making vacation plans, why not schedule your beach house Saturday-to-Saturday instead of Sunday-to-Sunday!" You may think that's silly, but I know from experience that even when I miss two Sundays in a row with my local church family because I am ministering in Africa, I am a bit out of sorts when I return. We need each other, thus the New Testament admonition, "not forsaking the assembling of ourselves together, as is the manner of some, but exhorting one another, and so much the more as you see the Day approaching." (Hebrews 10:25)

Stewardship of Morals

The second area we must be faithful stewards over is the area of our morals. I believe this will take at least two directions. First, I encourage those who are hoping to join Antioch to be faithful to keep a clear conscience.

Paul said it like this, in his instructions to a young pastor:

"This charge I commit to you, son Timothy, according to the prophecies previously made concerning you, that by them you may wage the good warfare, having faith and a good conscience, which some having rejected, concerning the faith have suffered shipwreck…" (1 Timothy 1:18-19)

There's a powerful combination for you. Forget the one-two punch of George Foreman or Muhammad Ali. There is nothing more formidable than the one-two powerhouse of faith and a good conscience! By them, we may wage the good warfare. Without either or both, our warship is headed for a wreck that will render it useless, possibly even bringing shame to the Commander, Himself. One of the truths that I stress with any potential new member of our church is the necessity of keeping a clear conscience. That takes many different forms. We keep a clear conscience by not walking in any sin, but quickly confessing it when we stumble. "But if we walk in the light, as He is in the light, we have fellowship with one another, and the blood of Jesus Christ His Son cleanses us from all sin." (1 John 1:7) We must be ruthlessly honest and intentional with ourselves about our own sin. Remember! "The heart is deceitful above all things, and desperately wicked. Who can know it?" (Jeremiah 17:9). The Lord answers His own question there, saying "I, the Lord, search the heart, I test the mind." Part of being a healthy member of a growing, vibrant fellowship of believers is being quick to run to the Lord with our sins, confess them to Him, and allow Him to cleanse us. Had Achan done that after he had taken the Babylonian garment, the gold and the silver during the battle of Jericho, then perhaps there would have been thirty-six fewer widows in Israel. Achan's sin led to defeat at Ai. He tried to hide something from God and from his brothers in the army, and it brought defeat and shame. (Joshua 7) Who knows? Maybe Achan's conscience was pierced by what he had done but he was too ashamed to talk to anyone about it until it was too late and he was forced to confess. We might feel shame about our own sins. That is precisely *why* we need help from our brothers and sisters, and that is one reason we *need* to be in a church and in close relationship with our fellow believers. Keep a clear conscience through confession of sins. It is vital.

The second way we "keep a clear conscience" is by keeping short accounts with our fellow believers. Think about it. My conscience cannot be clear if I am sinning against God in any way. It also cannot be clear if I am sinning against anyone created in God's image in any way! My relationship with the image-bearers of God will directly influence my own spiritual health and well-being, which in turn will directly influence the health and well-being of the church. How many of you have been in a church that was turned into living torment by a few people or families who stirred up dissension and strife like it was their job! If one bad apple can spoil the bushel basket, then surely one embittered soul can wreak havoc over an entire congregation. I encourage all potential members of Antioch to commit to always being a part of the solution to relational problems, not a part of the problem. That means that they must commit to going quickly to a brother who has offended them, following the steps laid out for us by the Lord in Matthew 18. That also means that they make a commitment to refrain from listening to or sharing gossip of any kind. "Let no corrupt word proceed out of your mouth, but what is good for necessary edification, that it may impart grace to the hearers." (Ephesians 4:29)

My mom tells the story of taking a drink from one of those little 6 oz. Cokes years ago and instantly making a face and spitting out the drink. She then poured the Coke out only to discover half a cigar, well-chewed, in the bottom of the bottle. How many would want to take a swig of that Coke? Or, imagine that you find a broccoli casserole on the counter, scoop some on a plate, take a big bite and then notice, as you are chewing, that the rest of the casserole on your plate is...moving! It is crawling with activity and about that time someone comes into the room and is horrified that you are eating this casserole that has been sitting out all weekend and good for nothing except the garbage.

That's the meaning of Paul's admonition in Ephesians 4:29. A Christian should no more allow a rotten word to proceed *out* of his mouth than he would allow a piece of rotten food or cigar-marinated Coke to proceed *into* his mouth! If it is disgusting to us coming in, Paul says it should be even more disgusting to us going out. Not only that, Paul goes on to say that such putrid language grieves the Holy Spirit.

Keeping a clear conscience, then, will require us to maintain short accounts, setting a guard at our lips, and being quick to ask forgiveness when we stumble.

The second part of stewarding our morals involves submission to authority. In my book, *Family-Integrated Church*, I spend an entire chapter on the responsibility the members of the congregation have to their elders. Let me give a brief synopsis here. First, the members of the church must **recognize** their leaders.

And we urge you, brethren, to recognize those who labor among you, and are over you in the Lord and admonish you… (1 Thessalonians 5:12)

That simply means that they are to be appreciated, held in high regard for their labor. Second, the church members must "esteem them highly."

…and to esteem them very highly in love for their work's sake. Be at peace among yourselves. (1 Thessalonians 5:13)

This takes it up a step, from appreciation to recognizing their leadership. To esteem someone is to make a decision with your mind that you will recognize his place of leadership and authority.

Not only that, but the writer of Hebrews encourages the flock to…

"Remember those who rule over you, who have spoken the word of God to you, whose faith follow, considering the outcome of their conduct." (Hebrews 13:7).

This speaks to the responsibility those in the congregation have to recognize that God has placed men in positions of leadership who should be remembered in prayer, and who are to be followed, and whose lives can be used as example of the faith. That is scary territory for any of us in leadership, but we must be willing to accept that as coming with the job.

Then the writer of Hebrews goes even further in describing the congregation's role with regard to the elders, requiring us to **obey** and **be submissive** to them:

Obey those who rule over you, and be submissive, for they watch out for your souls, as those who must give account. (Hebrews 13:17)

The first word the writer to the Hebrews uses is "obey," and the word literally means "to obey, to listen to, or to follow." I have to hear something in order to obey it. When Solomon asked God for wisdom, he literally asked for an "understanding heart," or a "heart that hears." That's what the writer of *Hebrews* is getting at. The church that hears the leaders' heart and vision with understanding will be MUCH more likely to take the next step and submit.

The second word the writer to the Hebrews uses is "submit," and the word literally means "to yield, to surrender, to cease to fight, to defer to."

John Chrysostom, a church father, wrote, "Anarchy then is an evil, and a cause of ruin, but no less an evil also is disobedience to rulers. For it comes again to the same. For a people not obeying a ruler is like one who has none; and perhaps even worse."

I had lunch with a man who joined our church recently, and while at the restaurant I ran into another local pastor. "How's the church going, brother?" I asked him. "Is it booming?" He replied, "Well, I wouldn't say it was booming," and I could see some pain in his face. I said, "Holding your own?" He smiled, kind of a tired smile and said, "Yeah. We just came through some inner turmoil." We talked for a few minutes and my heart went out to this man who, I could see, had just been through a battle. Sometimes the battles we pastors go through are our own fault; we have led poorly or not at all. We have been selfish shepherds. But many times the battles are because we are serving selfish sheep. Selfish *stubborn* sheep! Part of an orientation to a church for a new member must include a biblical discussion about the necessity of submission to authority. Otherwise we invite people into the fellowship who are like the woman who told her pastor that she didn't even want to go to heaven. "Why not?" he exclaimed, eyebrows raised in surprise. "Because," she said, "I read in Revelation there's going to be 24 elders there. I'd just as soon not go if I have to be around any more *elders*!"

Stewardship of Money

Daily Walk offers the following excerpt:

John G. Wendel and his sisters were some of the most miserly people of all time. Although they had received a huge inheritance from their parents, they spent very little of it and did all they could to keep their wealth for themselves. John was able to influence five of his six sisters never to marry, and they lived in the same house in New York City for 50 years. When the last sister died in 1931, her estate was valued at more than $100 million. Her only dress was one that she had made herself, and she had worn it for 25 years.

The Wendels had such a compulsion to hold on to their possessions that they lived like paupers. Even worse, they were like the kind of person Jesus referred to "who lays up treasure for himself, and is not rich toward God" (Luke 12:21).

The last thing on the list of things to talk about with prospective members is money. Not because it is the least important. To the contrary, Jesus made it clear that how we spend our money is an indication of our faithfulness as a steward in bigger areas as well. He said, "He who is faithful in what is least is faithful also in much; and he who is unjust in what is least is unjust also in much. Therefore if you have not been faithful in the unrighteous mammon, who will commit to your trust the true riches?" (Luke 16:10-11)

I encourage each prospective member of the church to be a giver. They shouldn't give because they think God needs the money; He owns the cattle on a thousand hills. He owns it all and has no needs whatsoever! They don't need to give because the church needs the money. God will provide for His work wherever it is being done in His name and in His way. I always tell new members that the main reason they need to give is because their heavenly Father is a giver; He gave His only Son to die in their place. He gives grace to His people every single day. He gave the breath you just breathed into your lungs. If we are going to be like God, then we need to learn to give. Not only that, there is plenty of biblical support for regular, sacrificial, voluntary giving. God taught His people in the Old Testament to always give the first fruits, a tenth of their increase. He even said that if they would give to Him, He would "rebuke the devourer" (protection from what *could* happen) and He would "open for you the windows of heaven and pour out for you such a blessing that there will not be room enough to receive it" (provision for what *does* happen and for every other need we have). God will be in debt to no man! If we give out of an obedient heart, God will bless His people, provoke them to give thanks and to praise Him, and He will receive the glory. (see 2 Corinthians 9:7-11)

I always tell new members in the class that I believe the tithe that was instituted in the Old Testament was not nullified in the New Testament. If anything, the principle under grace is to give freely, to give sacrificially, to give with a cheerful heart! I also tell the new members that I will not know how much they are giving. That information is between them and God and the only persons in the church who will know their giving patterns will be the two men who take care of the income and the outgo of funds. The only time someone's giving comes into my radar screen is if they have come to me for counseling and I realize that money is a root problem in their lives that must be dealt with.

I have never known a generous Christian who is following the Lord with all his heart in his giving to be in deep crisis in his marriage or with his job or with his finances. Those who have "transferred ownership" of all that they have to the Lord have probably done the same with their heart, with their tongue, with their thoughts, with their appetites. They are living a godly life and how they give is just one of the many fruits that is evidence of that life. May their tribe increase, to God's glory!

Chapter Seven

Where Will We Meet?

In the summer of 2007, my friend Rob and I traveled to Africa…

We pulled up to a store in a rural area of Zimbabwe, many miles from the nearest town of any size. On the way from Victoria Falls, which was now many hours and dusty kilometers ago, our vehicle had passed by hundreds of people standing or sitting by the road at various outposts or villages. Normally there would be a bus to come and pick them up and take them where they want to go. But not now. There is a fuel shortage in the country and transportation is a luxury afforded only by a few.

There is also a food shortage. We looked into the place that proudly advertised on a sign overhead, "Convenience and Bottle Store." The first part may have been true. It was a convenient place to pull over, and maybe the folks living in this out of the way place have found this in the past to be the store with all they need. But not now. The shelves were empty. The owner shook his head when our Zimbabwean escort asked about bottled water, rice, beans, or anything else we could take with us to our destination. We journeyed on and found the same story every place we stopped.

Rob and I were on our way to speak at a convention in the town of Manjolo. There would be hundreds of people in attendance, many of whom would walk for four or five hours to get there. Some walked for two days, so hungry were they for the Word of God. They would sleep on concrete floors in cinderblock school buildings during the week. They would gather under two huge trees and sit from nine o'clock in the morning until nine in the evening. They would eat sadsa, the staple food made of maize 'flour' and water.

And they would worship God in the most exuberant and refreshing way I have ever experienced. Singing at the tops of their lungs, they would leap and dance in such a way that huge clouds of dust rose up and danced with them. The lack of food and water, the uncomfortable sleeping conditions, the heat, the bugs, and the crowds did nothing to dampen their enthusiasm to celebrate the risen Savior. When we stood up to speak, they applauded wildly, not for us but for the opportunity they were about to experience; to hear someone preach the Word of God to them. They would listen patiently as the interpreter spoke our words in their native tongue, Tonga. They would take notes, flipping through their Bibles to every passage mentioned. And when the message ended, they would bow their heads and pray.

There was one moment during the week that made me tremble. Dozens of church leaders were standing at the front, having responded to an invitation by the local pastor. He turned and asked me to speak a word of encouragement to them, and my mind went to the book of Esther, the story of a young Jewish woman who became Queen of Persia at the same time there was a plan to destroy all of the Jewish people. Mordecai said to her, "Who knows whether you have come to the kingdom for such a time as this?" I challenged them that God has brought them to a place of leadership at such a time as this, when the stability of their nation stands on the brink. As I spoke, some of the people began to weep and then to wail. They were crying for their country and they were crying out to God for strength and wisdom and for help.

You may have glossed over it, but I tell you that story because it clearly paints a picture of a healthy church meeting under a grove of trees. There was no air conditioning. There were no pews. There was no comfortable fellowship hall, complete with commercial kitchen. There was no steeple, no church bus, and no 'welcome center' offering up coffee and doughnuts to early arrivals.

Don't get me wrong. None of those things that were missing in Zimbabwe are bad in and of themselves. But the church is not a place, it is a gathering of God's people, His "called-out ones," His ecclesia. I have two good friends who are leaders in a different church in town. We get together for lunch at least once a week and talk about what the Lord is doing in our lives, problems in our churches, whatever is on our minds that day. When they used to call my cell phone to see if I wanted to go to lunch, they would ask "Are you at the church?" I often answered, "No, but I am at the building." Or when someone finds out I am a pastor and asks me, "Where is your church?" sometimes I will tease them with, "Well, let's see…the church is at Kernodle Clinic working as a foot doctor, at the sign company, at the high school teaching math, at the construction site building a house…" The church is not a building, nor is it a service. It is the people of God who are called together to be part of His body, serving one another and reaching out to a lost community in the name of the Lord.

Where does the church meet? Well, everywhere. We met in a mission organization's building for the first several years of our existence, a converted grocery store. Then we moved to a college campus and moved our equipment there every Sunday for the worship service! We have met at an elementary school, in a fine arts studio, even in a shelter at the city park. Since 2002, we have met in a "traditional church building," although that description is a bit of a misnomer. Any building that houses the people of God for a corporate worship service is a "church building," at least during that hour or two.

The church can even meet in houses, and many do. But I would share one caution about 'house churches.' In my opinion, and this is simply my opinion, I believe a group of believers should only meet in a home for one of two reasons: security or size. There are some who meet in homes all around the world because they are part of the "underground church" for security reasons. They simply cannot meet in public places for fear of being dragged off to prison or worse. There are others who meet in a home because there are only 3-5 families starting the church, and they want to conserve resources and grow by 2 or 3 more families before they find a public place to rent, borrow, or buy. In other words, their "house meeting" is a temporary situation, kind of like the tabernacle in the wilderness. When the people of God were being moved about for 40 years in the wilderness, they had to construct a temporary place to worship God. The tabernacle was quickly replaced with permanent places of worship once the children of Israel came into the Promised Land. They were settled and a temporary place of worship was no longer necessary.

The problem with many 'house churches' is that they start with, or very quickly develop an "us four and no more" mentality. They have no vision for touching the world with the Gospel, though I am sure that is not their stated intention. They are simply in retreat mode, pulled into a secure location where they can do church "the way we want to do it." They are looking for security, but it is not because their lifestyle has been challenged by the authorities, like those believers in North Korea might be challenged. It is often because their sensibilities have been offended, or their feathers have been ruffled, and so they pull down the shades and start a church that they think will perfectly meet their desires. Sadly, most of these churches do not grow. They simply maintain, and sometimes they shrink even smaller until they dissipate altogether. Not only that, but as I said in *Family-Integrated Church*, it doesn't take more than one person to have a problem.

That's right. As long as there is one person in the church, there will be conflict. You have heard the story of the man, perhaps, who was stranded by himself on a deserted island for seven years. When he was finally found, he showed his rescuers around the island. They noticed he had built three huts for himself, and asked him what they were for.

"This one is where I live," he said, pointing to the first hut. "This one is where I go to church," pointing to the third hut.

"What's the other hut for?" the rescuers asked.

"That's where I *used* to go to church."

Having said all that, I know of some healthy churches that started meeting in a home and quickly outgrew the space. They started with a view to be a biblical church, to feed the flock and nurture them. Healthy sheep will reproduce, it's a given. When healthy sheep begin to tell other sheep about the good pasture they are in, the other sheep are attracted to that because, let's face it, there is a great dearth of healthy biblical churches now. That's one of the reasons why you are reading this book and even *considering* planting a new church!

Here are some possibilities for church locations:

Civic centers, daycare centers, movie theatres, schools, college campuses, restaurants that are closed on Sundays, Seventh Day Adventist church buildings, Moose Lodges (or other clubhouses), and of course, retail space (storefronts). The advantage of the storefront is that it becomes your space 24/7. You can use it for mid-week prayer, Men's Bible studies, homeschool co-op meetings, evangelism training, or anything else. The disadvantage is the cost. If you can find a Christian retailer in your area who has some space available he would let you use for a discounted price, that would be a blessing. A new church needs to keep her overhead as low as possible and move into larger, more expensive places only when she can afford them. Also, always try to negotiate a short-term lease, if the space only allows for a 50% increase or so in attendance. If you lock into a 5-year lease and then you outgrow the space and need another, you may be in a bind.

Our church began in 1987, meeting in the afternoon and sharing space with another church that met there Sunday morning, and Sunday and Wednesday evenings. We had our mid-week prayer service in the same space on Thursday evenings, and home groups met on various nights. There are a number of advantages to a Sunday afternoon service, including inexpensive (or free!) rent. There are also disadvantages to an afternoon service, including grumpy kids (and sometimes, adults). If you are trying to reach families, asking them to come and worship when it is time for their little ones to be napping is a difficult proposition. But it can certainly serve as a stopgap measure until another space becomes available or affordable. Our little church grew quickly, from 25 people to 125 in a little more than a year, even though we were meeting in the afternoon.

There are almost endless possibilities for housing a new church plant. If you approach the need for a place to meet with the attitude that God may do something completely outside of the 'norm,' I think you will be in a good place. No matter *where* that place is!

Chapter Eight

What's in a Name?

I don't know about you, but I probably wouldn't call "Stumpy's Tree Service" if I was looking for someone to come and take down a 60 foot oak tree in my front yard. Something about that just gives me cold chills. I also would probably skip right past a church in the yellow pages that was named "First Apostolic Church of the Most Holy Saints," if I was in the market, as they say. First, that name sounds a bit presumptuous, don't you think? Second, it sounds man-centered. I don't want to go to a church where it's all about the people. I want to be a part of a church that is all about the Lord.

Here are some names of real churches out there that made me laugh:

Divide Baptist Church
Fakes Chapel United Methodist Church
Agenda United Methodist Church
Boring United Methodist Church
Grassy Butte United Methodist Church
Deaf Missionary Baptist Church
Apistodookee United Methodist Fellowship
Steve's Church of Christ
Cowboy Church On Fire
Fire Baptized Holiness Church of God of the Americas

Makes you wonder, doesn't it?

Now don't get me wrong. A church can have the 'perfect' name, whatever that is, and be as dry and dusty as the potsherd Job used to scrape his sores. The name does not make the man; neither does it make the church. But the name *should* be a first indicator as to what this church is all about for those who are looking for a church to visit. That's why, when the five Antioch families started talking about names for their new church to be planted in June of 2008, they quickly got to a short list. They decided that their church name would begin with either Cornerstone or Shepherd's. Here is an excerpt from one of the elder's emails, as the group worked through this process:

Hi, everyone.

I would like to share some notes about the church names from which we have to choose. I could not be happier with the options before us. All of them are good names, in my opinion. I could be happy with any of them.

Interestingly, our favorite beginnings-of-the-name both refer to Jesus – Cornerstone and Shepherd's.

- **Cornerstone** – My mom's earlier email pointed out several passages related to this name. If we adopt it, we are saying that we are "members of God's household," being built on "the foundation of the apostles and prophets, with Christ Jesus himself as the chief cornerstone." (Eph. 2:19-22). The part about "foundation of the apostles and prophets" is appropriate – that's the New and Old Testaments, respectively – solid Bible teaching is an important part of what we all hope for in the new church. We understand that all the Scripture begins, ends, and points to Christ (the cornerstone part).

For me, the name Cornerstone brings to mind the words **solid**, **strength**, **righteous**, **well-grounded**.

- **Shepherd's** – I thought Laura did a good job explaining why Shepherd's is a good name. Jesus referred to himself as the Good Shepherd, who "lays down his life for the sheep." (John 10). By calling the church Shepherd's Something-Or-Other, we are acknowledging that this local church is Christ's and we are dependent on Him. It also has a nice tie to the elder form of governance – since Peter calls on the elders to be shepherds of God's flock. (Of course, more importantly, Jesus is the Chief Shepherd – thus the possessive form Shepherd's.)

  For me, the name Shepherd's brings to mind **peace**, **pastoral**, **dependence**, **still waters**.

  I was surprised that "Shepherd's" is not often used for churches. There are lots of "Good Shepherd..." but not as many "Shepherd's..." Most of the churches with Shepherd in the name seem to come from the Anglican and Episcopalian tradition. "Shepherd's Family Fellowship" returns no matching pages on Google.

They decided on Cornerstone Bible Church after much prayer and discussion.

We chose Antioch Community Church for our name in 1987 when we started the church plant for these simple reasons: we like the fact that the church at Antioch in Acts 13 was governed by a plurality of elders who were from different ethnic backgrounds. We liked that they were Spirit-led, as is evidenced by the fact that the Holy Spirit was able to get their attention about the matter of sending out missionaries. We liked the fact that they were missions-minded to the degree that they would be *willing* to listen to the Lord and send out two of their leaders! We chose Community to follow Antioch because we wanted to be non-denominational and committed to reaching our community with the Gospel of Jesus Christ. We chose "Church" to finish our name (rather than Fellowship or some other) simply because that's what Jesus called all of us who belong to Him. ***I will build my church, and the gates of Hades will not prevail against it…*** (Matthew 16:18).

Choosing the name of your church plant will not guarantee its success. Only the Lord will be able to do that. It is an important step, however, in defining who you are and what you believe.

Chapter Nine

What about Women?

One of the issues you will have to deal with as you prepare to plant a family-integrated church will be the role of women. In the 'liberal church,' this is not an issue. Women in many mainline churches can be pastors and elders, not because those churches have found a loophole in the Scriptures that the rest of us simply cannot find, but because they have chosen to ignore the clear teaching of Scripture and have caved to the pressures of the culture. In the evangelical churches, like the ones that *may* be helped by this book, it is an issue because the role of women in the church can become very divisive, very fast.

Let me say first that I am clear on the position of women who have been converted by the Holy Spirit: they are in Christ, right beside their brothers in the faith. They are not standing on a lower rung of the ladder, if you will, but are partakers of the faith in the same way that men are. Ephesians 1:3, ***Blessed be the God and Father of our Lord Jesus Christ, who has blessed us with every spiritual blessing in the heavenly places in Christ,*** applies to every single man, woman, and child who is *in* Christ. That's what Paul is saying, clearly, in Galatians 3:28: ***There is neither Jew nor Greek, there is neither slave nor free, there is neither male nor female; for you are all one in Christ Jesus.*** But here's where it gets tricky for those who take a liberal approach to

Scripture; taken out of context, you can use Galatians 3:28 to promote the teaching that women are just as qualified as men to serve as elders or pastors. The context of that verse, however, is clearly salvation, not roles or functions in church leadership. The preceding verse frames the context clearly: ***For as many of you as were baptized into Christ have put on Christ.*** (Gal. 3:27) You cannot wrench that verse out of its context and make it serve another purpose not intended for it—the support for women elders, for example. At least, you cannot do so with integrity. Women are equal to men with regard to salvation. Women are given gifts of the Spirit just like men are. Women are accepted in the beloved just like men are. Women are co-heirs with Christ, just like men are! But that's not the issue that has divided churches and even denominations. The divisive issue among many is whether women can exercise authority over men in the church. To make Paul say that women can lead men, using Galatians 3:28 as your pretext, is to make Paul a liar in 1 Timothy 2:12, where he says, ***And I do not permit a woman to teach or have authority over a man, but to be in silence.***

But even that is not the issue I want to discuss in this chapter. I would venture to say that if you picked this book up to read it, and you have made it *this* far, you probably believe like I do on this: that Scripture calls men to lead their families and the church. The question is, what *do* you believe about how much women should do in the church, especially in the context of the Sunday morning worship service?

It is my understanding that in the family-integrated church, there are two camps on this question of women in the Sunday morning service. One camp forbids a woman to speak in the Sunday morning service at all. Some churches (though not most) in this camp even forbid a woman to sit with her husband: she and the children sit on one side of the meeting place and the men sit on the other. That's one camp. The other camp would allow a woman to stand up in the public meeting on Sunday morning and share a testimony. Or read a Bible verse and tell what God has spoken to her heart about it that week. Or give thanks for her husband and children or publicly acknowledge a birthday in her family. Families sit together in these churches, which is a beautiful illustration in itself of what family-integrated worship is at its core.

Can you tell which camp I belong to? Members of the other camp would call me a liberal because I allow women to speak in the service. They might say that I don't believe part of the Bible is true, or that I ignore part of the truth of the Bible, because the Apostle Paul said a woman should "be in silence." Let me say that in my 21 years of pastoring the same church, we have had occasions that I could count on one hand when someone stood in our public meeting on Sunday morning during our open mic time and shared something that was inappropriate or unbiblical or just plain wrong. In each case, it was dealt with by the elders and correction was made so the people knew what the truth was. On the other hand, I cannot tell you how many <u>hundreds</u> of times people have stood up on Sunday morning and shared something that was so clearly from the Lord, that honored His name, that benefitted the body, that caused the faith of those in the meeting place to grow. Sometimes those things were shared by women. There is a freedom at Antioch to stand up and share what the Lord is doing, and I cherish that freedom. It has made us a better church. It has made us a healthier people. It has pointed people to the grace of the Lord Jesus Christ.

But not only that. We don't practice such things at Antioch because "they work," but because we believe they are biblical. The verb tense that is used in 1 Timothy 2:12, "And I do not permit a woman to teach" is present infinitive active. Paul is saying, "I do not permit a woman to teach continuously," or to usurp the authority of men. The issue there is authority and a woman's God-given role to submit to her husband's authority at home and in the church. It is clear from 1 Corinthians 11:2-16 that it was perfectly fine for women to pray or prophesy in the church at Corinth. The issue was not whether she could open her mouth but whether she was honoring her husband as her authority. It is clear from Acts 21:9 that Philip, one of the "seven," had four daughters who prophesied. Where did they prophesy? Again, Scripture is clear that prophesy was a gift given to edify the body, to build up the church, so it stands to reason that Philip's daughters used their gift in the public meetings.

Wayne Grudem, in his classic book *Systematic Theology*, writes this:

> In this section (1 Corinthians 14:33-36) Paul cannot be prohibiting all public speech by women in the church, for he clearly allows them to pray and prophesy in church in 1 Corinthians 11:5. Therefore, it is best to understand this passage as referring to speech that is in the category being discussed in the immediate context, namely, the spoken evaluation and judging of prophecies in the congregation. (p. 939)

I like the way Grudem defines the term, "prophesy," as it is used by Paul in the New Testament. He says it is not "authoritative Bible teaching...but rather reporting something which God spontaneously brings to mind."

OK, so what does this have to do with you? Nothing, if everyone in your church plant core group believes the same way about the role of women in the church. If you are all in the first camp, and women will not be allowed to speak, then I appeal to you to reconsider, based on the evidence of Scripture. If you are all in the second camp, and will allow the women in your church to pray or 'prophesy,' then there is nothing you have to do either, except this. Put it in writing as part of your statement of beliefs. Include it as part of your teaching in the New Members Class. It will come up, and if you start out knowing what you believe and why you believe it, and you have a document that states it clearly, then you may be saved some future grief!

Chapter Ten

What, NO Programs?!

Allow me to insert another excerpt from my book *Family-Integrated Church* here, as it relates to the topic of programs. I have updated it:

I remember hearing years ago about how a wall-eyed pike could be conditioned into unbelief. You see, the pike's favorite food is a minnow. You drop a minnow in a tank with a pike, and it is time for a minnow funeral. An experiment was conducted where a glass partition was put in the tank, dividing it in half, with the pike on one side and the minnow on the other. At first, the pike took off after that minnow like a preacher after a piece of fried chicken. The pike slammed into the glass! Undaunted, the pike got up a full head of steam, licking his chops in anticipation of a fish fry, and wham! He hit the glass again. And then again. And again. Finally, he gave up. His little fish brain had been reprogrammed to believe a lie: "I can't eat minnows anymore. It hurts like crazy whenever I try. Just can't do it."

Then the proof that the conditioning was complete; the glass partition was removed. The minnow swam cautiously, slowly towards the pike, knowing his little life was a nano-second away from being a distant memory. He swam closer to his predator. No response. The pike didn't even give the minnow a look. Why should he? He believed he couldn't have it, so why torment himself by eyeballing the tasty morsel? The truth had not changed; the pike *could* eat the minnow. However, he now suffered from unbelief, and went hungry because of it. He had believed a lie.

I know we humans are much higher up the food chain. Hey, we EAT the pike that eats the minnow (or wishes he had)! The truth is, however, that we can be conditioned into believing a lie just as easily, and I believe the church today has believed LOTS of them.

I believe one of those lies says, "A healthy church is a program-driven church." We can see the evidence of this lie all around as churches compete with one another to have the most programs to offer the community. The winning church is the one that has something every night for the people to do, keeps them hustling off to this meeting or to that event, and brags that they are "running 400 in Sunday School."

I like to have fun with pastors; we tend to be a very insecure bunch. I was at a pastors' conference once and a fellow pastor I had just met asked me, "So, how many are you running in Sunday School?" I didn't crack a smile; in fact, I frowned and said, "Oh, we really discourage running at church, during Sunday School or anytime. Someone could get hurt." There was a slight pause as I saw this pastor trying to figure out which planet I had beamed in from. Then he chuckled nervously and said, "Ha! That was a good one."

After another pause, he said it again, "So, how many ARE you running in Sunday School?" I smiled this time and said, "We don't have Sunday School." Now he was convinced that there was something wrong with me and pursued his line of questioning until he got the answer he wanted: how many people we have (which happened to be fewer than his number). Satisfied that his church was superior, he felt free to challenge me on Sunday School. I simply told him that at Antioch, we believe our primary responsibility is to train fathers to love and lead their families, and Sunday School can sometimes interfere with that. I didn't even broach the subject of age-segregation and the problems it causes.

A program can accomplish a specific task; there is no doubt about it. The problem is that many programs accomplish that task and are no longer needed, but because the people have been conditioned to believe that the program is vital to their spiritual growth and well-being, then it must be continued at all costs! What began perhaps as a movement of God quickly becomes a monument and finally a memorial. There is no life there but like a perpetual care cemetery, that program must be trimmed and maintained forever.

Most of us may know that Sunday School began in England in the 1700's and the idea spread to the United States and caught on in the 1800's. But why was Sunday School started in the first place? It was an effort to reach out to the poor children who were not well-educated, who were running wild in the streets on the "Sabbath" and profaning the day of the Lord. It was an effort at evangelism and education, and I believe God used the effort to win souls and encourage saints to reach out. But as with many programs that started out with good intentions, the purpose morphed into a place to corral young people and children so they could be kept out of trouble and possibly where they could be taught the Bible stories that every child should know.

Am I suggesting that any church that offers a Sunday School program is outside the will of God and therefore disobedient? No, I will not make that judgment. I would say, however, that many churches who offer age-segregated programs do so because they believe that is 'normal Christianity,' not necessarily because they believe it is the best way to reach children. Many keep the programs in place because of the same old refrain that we have heard since time immemorial: "We have *always* done it that way." Their church motto may be, "As it was in the beginning, is now, and forever shall be. Amen." Some keep Sunday School and other programs in place because they honestly believe that a church without a Sunday School program is not even a biblical church. But I would challenge them to find anything that vaguely resembles age-segregation in the Scripture. The burden of proof is on those who maintain age-segregation in the church, not on those who do not.

That kind of talk usually brings up the next question. 'Do you mean to tell me that your church never has *any* programs?!'

The answer is 'no.' We offer programs, but they are for a season and targeted to a specific purpose that has a beginning, a middle and an end. For example, we like to have a summer reading program at Antioch, and encourage the children and young adults (ages 2-18) to read Christian classics, read their Bible daily, and memorize sections of Scripture. Obviously the non-readers have to have the Bible read to them, but they can still participate, and you would be surprised at how quickly a 3 year-old can memorize Scripture! At the end of the summer, we have a recognition service on a Sunday afternoon picnic at the park and give rewards to those who have faithfully hidden God's Word in their hearts. Many of our teens, for example, have memorized Romans 8, Matthew 5-7, and much more. Several memorized all of 2 Timothy in the summer of 2006.

Now, this "program" has been successful on many levels. A young man testified in a service on Sunday morning that it was the "Summer Reading Program" that got him interested a few years back in reading his Bible on a daily basis. Does that mean, then, that we must do the reading program every year? Or, shouldn't we do it *year round*, since it is such a successful "program?" No, we would prefer to leave it up to the Lord one year at a time. We know the moment it becomes an "institution" of the church, some of its lifeblood will be drained away, and it can become a "tradition" of man rather than a movement of the Holy Spirit.

We have substituted people for programs, relationships for rituals. Instead of a Sunday School program, we have people on occasion who will come to the elders with an idea. "I want to offer a course in apologetics on Sunday morning before the worship service," three men proposed to the elders. The class was open to all ages, of course, and was offered for a season. It was not a program but an opportunity for these three men to sharpen their own thinking about how to defend the faith, and the rest of us got to learn along with them and got to know each other on a deeper level. The same is happening with the women, as there is a group meeting now and going through a study entitled "When Godly People Do Ungodly Things," by Beth Moore.

The women and their daughters (12 and up) go on a yearly 2-day retreat where relationships are nurtured and the older women invest in the younger through some practical teaching. The men go on an annual retreat also, and we always come back home with a renewed sense of purpose and vision as men and fathers who are called into battle side by side.

There are lots of musically gifted people in our church, and as the Bible says, "the Son can only do what He sees the Father doing" (paraphrase of John 5:19). So, there are lots of sons and daughters at Antioch who love to play and sing for God's glory. One year, three of the adults in the church who were a part of our worship team approached the elders with a request. "Could we meet with the young people who are interested and teach them about using music to worship the Lord?" We gave our blessing to the idea, and the young people began to meet with these three adults, and other parents, every Sunday after the morning service. They would eat together in a classroom while one of the adults taught from the Scriptures about what biblical worship is and how much God is interested in the heart of the worshiper. Then they would spend an hour together in the sanctuary, working on songs, drama, and even liturgical dance together.

Can there be programs in the church? Yes, but God works through people, not programs. Here's what E.M. Bounds said about it:

We are constantly on a stretch, if not on a strain, to devise new methods, new plans, new organizations to advance the Church and secure enlargement and efficiency for the gospel. This trend of the day has a tendency to lose sight of the man or sink the man in the plan or organization. God's plan is to make much of the man, far more of him than of anything else. Men are God's method. The Church is looking for better methods; God is looking for better men... When God declares that "the eyes of the Lord run to and fro throughout the whole earth, to show himself strong on behalf of those whose heart is loyal to Him," He declares the necessity of men and His dependence on them as a channel through which to exert His power upon the world.

What the Church needs today is not more machinery or better, not new organizations or more and novel methods, but men whom the Holy Ghost can use — men of prayer, men mighty in prayer. The Holy Ghost does not flow through methods, but through men. He does not come on machinery, but on men. He does not anoint plans, but men — men of prayer. (E. M. Bounds, Power through Prayer)

I would submit that there can be programs, but they must be initiated by the Holy Spirit and produced through prayer. Those who administrate them must work under the umbrella of God-given authority, and should be ready and expecting to bury the program when its purpose has been served. Otherwise, that program becomes an end in itself. When that happens, the whole church is turned upside down to the point that when a new family visits, the members salivate as they see "fresh meat" who will be able to *serve* their programs!

Programs can be wonderful servants but terrible taskmasters.

Chapter Eleven

Who You Gonna' Serve?

A church with no outreach exists only to serve itself. A church that exists only to serve itself is not a church at all. A church that is not a church at all should not even exist!

How's that for shocking language?

Many churches are like church programs. They were started with the greatest of intentions and for a while served a noble purpose. They met a need, even reached lost people and helped fulfill the Great Commission. But then something happened. Kind of like what happened to Congress when it discovered that it could pass laws that would serve its own ends rather than pass laws that would serve the greater good and protect the interests of the United States as a whole. If a Congress or a church exists for the sole purpose of self-sustenance, it is time for revival or revolution!

Don't get me wrong and run to the opposite extreme. I am not espousing a seeker-sensitive approach to church. I do not believe the church exists for the sole purpose of getting 'seekers' into the service or the building or even into the lives of the people who are *part* of the church! You want to read a "seeker-sensitive-buster" passage? Read the story of Ananias and Sapphira in Acts 5. You remember those two? They lied to the apostles about a generous donation they were making to the church, trying to pretend that they were giving *all* of the money they had made from the sale of their land. Peter asked them why they would lie to the Holy Spirit like that and first Ananias and then a few hours later Sapphira both dropped dead when their lie was exposed. Right there in front of God and the Apostles, they fell out. *Then*, check out the response of the 'seekers' and everybody else in town who did not believe in Jesus when they heard what was going on over there at "First Church @ Jerusalem": ***Yet none of the rest dared join them, but the people esteemed them highly.*** (Acts 5:13) In other words, everybody in town who was not in the church said, "You Christians go right ahead with your worship service this Sunday, you guys are GREAT, but, uh, I won't be able to make it this Sunday. That's right, I, uh, I just remembered, I am…sorting my socks that day! Yeah, that's it! And, uh, I, uh, the… goat-vet is coming by the house, too. Yep, time for a de-worming! Heh-heh. Can't put *that* off!"

Seeker-sensitive? Are you kidding me? Are you really going to turn a church into a seeker-sensitive shrine? Are you really going to jettison one of the primary purposes of the church to cater to those who are not a part of the church hoping that they will become a part of the church and then stay in the church and *not* be fed and *not* grow to maturity but somehow be able to help you reach out to other 'seekers' who are also not a part of the church? Hmmm? I know that's a long sentence and maybe hard to read aloud in one breath. But the seeker-sensitive movement is a long-*shot* and downright *impossible* to find in Scripture!

Am I saying that the church with a seeker-sensitive philosophy that is feeding the flock and growing a church toward maturity does not exist? No, I am sure that it does, but my guess is that such a church would be the exception, not the rule.

Ephesians 4:11-13 says it pretty clearly:

And He Himself gave some to be apostles, some prophets, some evangelists, and some pastors and teachers, for the equipping of the saints for the work of ministry, for the edifying of the body of Christ, till we all come to the unity of the faith and of the knowledge of the Son of God, to a perfect man, to the measure of the stature of the fullness of Christ...

What is Paul saying? Jesus Christ gave gifts to the church, people with certain gifts and abilities. Why? So the church could be equipped to do ministry. Why else? So the church could be built up, edified, matured. How much? Until the church becomes 'perfect,' even to the measure of the stature of the fullness of Christ. Now, the way I interpret that passage follows the old hermeneutic principle that says, "If the plain sense makes sense, seek no other sense, lest you find nonsense." And the plain sense is very plain: the church is to be equipped by its leadership to do ministry. The ministry that the body does is first of all to be focused on helping the body itself grow up to maturity. That's precisely what Paul and Peter said: ***As each one has received a gift, minister it to one another, as good stewards of the manifold grace of God.*** (1 Peter 4:10) Paul said, ***...speaking the truth in love, (we) may grow up in all things into Him who is the head – Christ – from whom the whole body, joined and knit together by what every joint supplies, according to the effective working by which every part does its share, causes growth of the body for the edifying of itself in love.*** (Ephesians 4:15-16)

The church that pours all its energies into reaching the lost is going to look around one day and wonder why the church is, as Vance Havner used to say, "A mile wide and an inch deep." It will look and sound like a nursery, probably, because most of the sheep who were not being equipped to do the work of ministry and not being taught the meat of the

Word so they could grow up will have gotten up and left! All that's left are the new lambs who have no one to care for them and bring them to maturity.

What is the best guarantee that a church will have biblical outreach, then? Ask anybody who has livestock and they will tell you: if you take care of the adult animals you have been given, and you keep them healthy, they *will* reproduce. Healthy sheep breed. Period. But unhealthy sheep do not.

The best kind of outreach for a church, then, is to make sure that its members are healthy, well-fed, cared for, and focused on the Lord Jesus Christ as the source of their life and health and strength! Again, one of the reasons our church is family-integrated is because we believe that healthy families make up a healthy church. The best way to insure you have healthy families is to train and equip the fathers to be the spiritual leader and discipler for his family.

Is that it? Just focus on the families in your church and forget about the lost and dying in the world? No. I would say that if that's all you are doing you are probably doing more than most churches who ignore Dads and the families to focus on reaching the seekers. In the long run, the church that helps families mature and grow will have a legacy for Christ, but there is more that needs to be done. Look at the story of the first church in Jerusalem. God scattered the apostles and sent them out to towns and cities, and the gospel was preached and new churches were planted everywhere they went. Look at the story of the church at Antioch again. God spoke to them and told them to do outreach that would go beyond the four walls of the church and even the four walls of the city. The greatest missionary journey in history took place as two men, Paul and Barnabus, were obedient to help fulfill the Great Commission, as the Holy Spirit directed (Acts 13). They did not go out on their own, they were *sent* out by the church they served. We must also be sending people out to do ministry in the city we live in and beyond.

One of the questions that is often asked of a family-integrated church is, "How do you do outreach?" There is not one answer that is the right one. There are many wrong answers, including the one that says "We are trusting God to reach the lost; we have been tasked only with discipling the ones we have here." That is not an obedient response to the Great Commission and should not ever represent the "Mission Program" of a church.

At Antioch, and at the churches we have planted and hope to plant in the future, we try to do outreach in several different ways.

First, we encourage the members of the church to *be* the ambassadors of reconciliation that they *are* (2 Corinthians 5:20). They hear regularly from the pulpit an exhortation to "Go into the world this week and tell people about Jesus, look for opportunities to be the salt of the earth and the light of the world." They also hear regular words of testimony during the Sunday service as people will stand and share about an encounter they had that week and how they are reaching out to the lost at work, in the community, in their extended family, and so on.

Second, we will organize periodic outreaches into the community. We have done several door-to-door campaigns in our neighborhood, trying to knock on every door within a one-mile radius of the church building, inviting the neighbors over for a hot dog supper. We have done other outreaches, including setting up sound equipment and singing at a trailer park, drawing a crowd, and then preaching the gospel to the listeners. We have done services at local parks and apartment complexes. We have had numerous picnics at parks and lakes in the area, and while there as a church, looked for opportunities to talk others in the park about Christ. We have stood on street corners, some of us, and handed out tracts and talked to people who would stop. We support local ministries that reach out to teens who suspect they are pregnant, or who minister to people on the street who are struggling with various addictions.

Third, we have at least one short term mission trip every year that folks in the church are encouraged to go on or participate with in some way. Many years we have had more than one trip. Our church has sent teams to Haiti, Kenya, Zimbabwe, Ghana, South Africa, India, Colombia, and other places over seas. I have conducted many pastors' conferences in African countries, with the help of various men from the church. We have also sent teams to do relief work in Mississippi after Hurricane Katrina, and other places of need in the U.S.

Fourth, we have always given a good amount of money to missionaries or church planters who are working in the states or in foreign countries. Since our birth in 1987, starting with 5 families, Antioch has been privileged to be able to give away nearly 20% of every dollar that has come in. That is a grace that has been given to us by the Lord and we give Him all the glory and honor. We know that there are many churches who give more, and I say 'bless you' if you are in one that does! The sad truth is, however, that the average church in America pays more every year in interest, to service its own debt, than it pays to foreign missions. That is sad and an argument against a church ever going into debt for anything, including a building! (more about this in Chapter 12)

Fifth, we challenge our folks to use their home groups for outreach. Many people will come to a home Bible Study before they will come to a Sunday morning church service, so we want to use that 'door' as a way to help people find an entrance into the Kingdom.

Sixth, this year we will offer a Mission Conference. We will bring in a former church member who is now the director of a ministry that has trained over thirty thousand pastors in Africa. We will spend a weekend together with him and other representatives of missions that we support, challenging and informing our own people about the great work these folks are doing. We are hoping, also, that God will bring in people who don't normally go to church or who don't know the Lord, but will come and hear men and women speak about what God is doing on the continent of Africa and around the world.

So I close this chapter with the way I started it: "Who you gonna' serve?" The church that is committed to serving itself will ultimately serve no one. The church that is committed to serving Christ by tending the flock of God that He brings in and by going out after the lost sheep and bringing them into the fold will be a blessed church indeed!

Chapter Twelve

What about Pastors, Pulpits, and Property?

Maybe this is too ambitious a title. To handle all three of those "P's" would be asking a lot. But I am not going to write much on each one, just share some of the basic understandings we have come to as a church.

Pastors

I believe in pastors for the local church. I am one. But I would remind my readers that a hierarchical model of leadership, where the pastor is the CEO at the top and the elders are the board of directors under him and the deacons are the senior management and the congregation is made up of worker bees…is simply a corporate model, not a biblical one, in my opinion. For a more detailed discussion of this, read my book *Family-Integrated Church*, especially Chapters Eleven and Twelve. I will simply say here that I like Alexander Strauch's teaching in his book *Biblical Eldership* that one man can be considered "first among equals" in the group of elders who lead a church. At Antioch, we call that man the pastor. I have no more authority than any of the other three elders, but I am the one God has raised up to lead the leaders. I am accountable to them and we share in all the decisions of importance. They trust me with the daily details, and I do not have to call an elder meeting to buy more paper at Office Depot. But I would not accept a speaking engagement or make any other plans which would affect the health of the body unless I first received permission from the elders.

My salary is set by the other elders and they will sometimes consult with the deacons or other godly men in the body when trying to decide on a salary raise or a benefit to offer. For nearly seventeen years I worked part-time as a college instructor, and that allowed the church to pay me a partial salary. I don't think there is anything wrong with a pastor being a 'tent-maker' as Paul was, but neither do I think it is more or less 'spiritual' to do so. The truth is, most pastors worldwide have to work another job to supplement what their churches are able to pay them, so I found myself in good company when I did the same. When the work of teaching 4 courses a semester began to erode my effectiveness in helping to oversee a growing flock, I went to the elders and asked if I could stop tent-making and focus all of my energies on helping to nurture the church. They said yes, and gave me a raise to allow me to do what I needed to do for the church without having an outside source of income. As I am writing this, the university has called and asked if I would come back to teach two half-semester courses in the spring of 2009. The elders and my wife have agreed, so I will be back on the college campus for a season, teaching a much-reduced load that should not impair my ability to serve the needs of the flock. What can I say? I like the challenge of being on the college campus, teaching students and impacting them for the Gospel. I also like being bi-vocational. It helps me to relate to my flock since I am 'in the world' like they are, working in sometimes difficult places and with difficult people.

The elders have also allowed me to hire my oldest son to come on staff part-time with me. Micah has a desire to be a pastor one day and so we are allowing him to apprentice under me while he also works on a seminary degree and works part-time in construction. My daughter Hannah also serves as the church secretary on a part-time basis, working 5-6 hours a week. This is only the second time in Antioch's 21 year history that we have had 'multiple staff,' and of course many pastors will laugh at the idea. Your church may have a staff of dozens, but most churches have a solo pastor and *maybe* a part-time secretary.

How do you go about hiring people to work on staff? Very carefully. My belief is that leadership comes from within and the best people to love the sheep are the shepherds. Not the hirelings. So, I would rather hire from within, putting people into paid staff positions who are already here, already doing the work of ministry without the salary, already committed to loving and serving the flock that they belong to. I realize that I have very little experience in this area, but the little that I do have has served to confirm my beliefs about hiring paid staff.

How do you fire a pastor? I have absolutely zero experience in this one. I have been the pastor of Antioch Community Church virtually since it began and have only hired two assistant pastors in our twenty-one years. The first assistant left to take a position in a larger church. The second assistant, my son, is still with me. My guess is that the way you fire a pastor would depend on the circumstances. If the need to let someone go arises out of a moral failure, then the goal would be to restore the brother to spiritual health, and that would mean keeping him on the payroll if possible while he goes through counseling. Of course, that would depend on the level of the offense and the depth of his repentance! If the moral failure is such that he cannot or should not continue, then a suitable amount of time ought to be given for him to find other employment.

If the need to remove an employee is the result of a different vision, then again the circumstances would dictate how it should be handled. If the pastor or the assistant in question is being divisive, attempting to "draw away the disciples after themselves," (Acts 20:30), it must be dealt with quickly and decisively. If the man simply has grown to favor a different way of 'doing church,' and the two visions are incompatible, then the separation can take more time and can even result in a church plant! Whatever the case, the Lord is able to give wisdom to all who lack it.

Pulpits

One of the items in our church's constitution reads, "The Pastor may occupy the pulpit without question; but if he should wish to bring in an outside speaker, he shall seek the advice and consent of the Elders." I preach 85% of the Sunday mornings in a typical year, with between 6 and 8 times filled by other men in the congregation. That doesn't mean that I take 6-8 weeks of vacation. I am usually on vacation with my family one Sunday out of the year, and on a mission trip two Sundays of the year. The other 3-5 Sundays I am generally at Antioch, but I am giving another man in the church an opportunity to preach. That is part of my son's apprenticeship training, for example, to preach about once a quarter. We will then sit down over lunch after a few days and talk through his sermon, discussing what he did well and what he can improve on. There are also discussions in the weeks leading up to his sermon, and I help him with the text, offer suggestions for the outline, the illustrations, or anything else he needs help with in preparation.

They say that a pastor's pulpit in America is one of the most jealously-guarded places in the world. The truth is, many pastors are afraid to ever allow anyone to fill their pulpit because of their insecurity and fear that the one who fills it would preach better than they do. Others are afraid to allow anyone else to preach because they are afraid new and strange doctrines might be taught. Or they fear incompetence in the pulpit would drive people away, or give visitors the wrong impression, or upset the 'pillars' of the church, or…the list goes on. The bottom line with all of this is fear, and the Bible is clear that we have not been given a spirit of fear. We must fear God, certainly, and we would never want to do anything intentionally to hurt His church. But let's face it: the only way a preacher learns to preach is by preaching. Just like a writer learns to write by writing and a public speaker learns to speak by speaking. Here is an excerpt from my book, *You* Can *Write!*

Good writers write every day. And most of it is BAD writing, but some of it is not! In his book, If You Want to Walk on Water, You Have to Get Out of the Boat, John Ortberg tells a story he found in another book entitled, Art and Fear. "A ceramics teacher divided his class into two groups. One group would be graded solely on quantity of work—fifty pounds of pottery would be an 'A,' forty would be a 'B,' and so on. The other group would be graded on quality. Students in that group had to produce only one pot—but it had better be good. **Amazingly, the highest quality pots were turned out by the quantity group."** (emphasis mine)

It seems that while the quantity group kept churning out pots, they were continually learning from their disasters and growing as artists. The quality group sat around theorizing about perfection and worrying about it—but they never actually got any better." And THAT'S why my wife and I have seven kids! We just keep trying to get it right…! Just kidding. But there IS a powerful principle at work here for writers. You learn to write by writing. LOTS of writing. Same with speaking. I used to have my students at the university give

SOME kind of speech just about every day. And at the end of the year, when they evaluated the course, many of them would say "I learned to speak, and to overcome my fear, by having to speak in class nearly every day." The students in my homeschool writing classes have to bring a paper to class every week, and read it out loud. This positive peer pressure makes them want to write better papers, and the writing and re-writing yields great results. A few years ago, our students entered a national contest sponsored by Josh McDowell. One of them won honorable mention in the contest, and one of them won the Grand Prize, which was a Dell Laptop! Two years ago, I had my students enter a local writing contest, and out of 9 prizes given for High School Fiction, High School Poetry, and Middle School Fiction, the students in my classes took 6 of them. They learned to write well enough to win contests by writing.

That illustrates my point, I hope: we need to give other men of God an opportunity to hone the gift that God has given them to preach. If we are "convulsively clinging to the pulpit," that opportunity will not be there. Having said that, we *are* called to protect the flock, and shepherd them with care. That means that we *do* guard the pulpit. If a man in the church tells me he thinks he is called to preach, I do not immediately schedule him for a Sunday morning sermon. He may be like the man who was convinced he was called to preach but every time he did so, the people would either be squirming in their seats, or falling asleep, or looking for any excuse they could find to slip out of the pew and go out to the foyer or the bathroom or check the stove at home! When this was gently pointed out to the man who thought he was called to preach, he replied, "Well, I am sure I have been called to preach; I guess these folks just aren't called to listen!" The truth is, if someone is truly called to preach, he will have listeners, and what he teaches will bear fruit. So, if brother

Joe wants to get up in the pulpit and preach, I will first give him some smaller tests. I will ask him to share at our home group. There is a much smaller crowd there, maybe 20-35 people, and much less potential for damage to the hearers *or* the speaker! I may ask him to speak at a Men's Breakfast. There are maybe 50-65 men and young men at those, but the atmosphere is casual and the men know that any one of their brothers may be standing up to address them; they do not come expecting a polished presentation. I may ask him to share his testimony in one of our meetings. The point is, the elders and I guard the pulpit by not allowing just anybody to have the 40-55 minute preaching slot.

There is always an open mic time at Antioch, and many of our men are very comfortable standing up and sharing something with the congregation, whether it is an illustration or a Bible passage that emphasizes something I preached that morning, or whether it is something else they feel led to share about. Just having that avenue every Sunday does two things, at least. First, it gives an opportunity for anyone in the body of Christ to minister a brief word of encouragement, or offer up a thanksgiving or a testimony. You know why that's important? Because Sunday morning service is not a spectator sport! It is not a show that features the leading characters, the pastor and the worship leader. It is a participatory event, featuring the Lord Jesus Christ who is enabling His supporting actors and actresses to speak the parts He has given them for that particular scene. You know what happens to a man who rarely or never gets to participate in a Sunday morning service of worship? He dries up or he blows up and leaves. So, giving the body a chance to be the body on Sunday morning is a huge blessing to the body and, I believe, brings honor to the Son.

Second, having that open mic time allows the Holy Spirit to complete the sermon that the pastor began. I have been overwhelmed at times by what the members of the congregation will speak to one another after I have finished preaching. There is insight there. I am not the sole recipient of the Holy Spirit or of wisdom from God's Word or knowledge of His ways. I am so thankful that the Lord has given the people at Antioch confidence that they can hear from God and they can share what they hear with the rest of us. Is that dangerous? Yes, there is the potential every time somebody opens his mouth, including me, that something wrong, even damaging, might be spoken. But do you want to know what the greater danger is? The greater danger happens when we make sure that no one but the 'trained professional' speaks. The danger there is that if he is wrong, no one will call him on it. If he is wrong, many will not even realize it because they have grown lazy and complacent in their own study of the Scriptures. Why should they study when they can just come and sit at the pastor's feet every week and soak up his teaching? Pretty soon, the pastor could say that Acts 2:38, ***Repent, and let every one of you be baptized in the name of Jesus Christ for the remission of sins; and you shall receive the gift of the Holy Spirit*** means that every single believer speaks in tongues and that if you don't speak in tongues then you are not saved. If the people in the pews are not students of the Word, if they have grown fat and lazy listening to their great leader, they will believe this deception and even begin to preach it themselves. If I tried to pull that stunt at Antioch, there would be at least a dozen people who would stand up after the sermon and ask me if I really meant that every believer speaks in tongues. Folks, listen. In 21 years, the open mic time has yielded about 3 times when someone stood up and said something that was off the wall or unbiblical or just plain off base. In each of those times, that person was gently corrected and the congregation was instructed as to the truth of the matter (see Chapter 2 of *Family-Integrated Church*, "A Strange Visitation"). But I cannot tell you how many *hundreds* of times members of the congregation have stood up and shared something powerful, something challenging, something encouraging, something touching or heartfelt, that has lined up with Scripture and has helped the church to mature. I could NOT have shared all of those things, nor would I have even known HOW to share all those things. We are a body, made up of different parts, and the body grows as the parts do what they are supposed to do.

Let me close this section with a final word about the pulpit: it is central to the health of the church. The Word of God is center stage, and so I believe there is something symbolic about moving the pulpit off center and preaching from the side rather than the center. I will not move the pulpit. I will also ask the members of the church to stand when we read the text for each Sunday, "out of honor for God's Word."

Finally, and this is crucial, the best preaching is expository. In fact, some would argue that the *only* preaching is expository! We are working through the book of Luke as I write this book. We started in September of 2007, one year ago, and we are now in chapter 11. I guess that means we will be in Luke for at least another year or two. Before Luke I preached through Ephesians. Before that? Joshua. You get the point. My belief is that there is no substitute for line upon line preaching through whole books of the Bible. It feeds the people with good, solid meat, while at the same time providing milk for the younger ones. You will also preach the *hard sayings* without making it obvious that you chose a hard saying because someone in particular in the body needed it. Finally, there is a benefit to the preacher *and* the people because you always know what the next text will be. I used to spend half the week searching the Scriptures and crying out to the Lord, just trying to choose the text. Now I know what I will be preaching months in advance, but I am also open to the Lord changing my direction for a Sunday or through the Christmas or Easter seasons, if need be.

Property

In Chapter 17 of *Family-Integrated Church*, I tell the story of how we got our church building. In a nutshell, God did it. The basic conviction that enabled us to be in a place where God *would* do it was a refusal to borrow money as a church. We would not go to the bank and become slaves to the lender, and instead we asked God to supply our needs. He did. We are in the middle of a ten year "lease to purchase agreement" with the church that owns our property. Every lease payment we have made has gone towards the purchase price of the building and land. There is no interest; every penny goes to paying off the principal. There is also no 'debt,' because we could walk away from the building without penalty of any kind, as long as we give the owners a 30-day notice. Do you see? We are paying off a piece of property without debt and without interest, without lawyers and without bankers. God has done a marvelous thing, and whenever I share the story in the New Members' Class, the people shake their heads in awe of our God.

Now, having said all of that, I realize that there are many out there who have no qualms whatsoever about their church borrowing money. That is entirely between you and God. If you are already in debt as a church, I would advise you to refinance to a 10 or 15-year, fixed mortgage, and then put extra toward the principle each month to try and pay off the building in half the time.

Besides a place to meet, there is also some equipment a church would be wise to purchase, unless there is a way to borrow it. When Cornerstone Bible Church started in Asheboro, NC, they borrowed an LCD projector, a screen, and a portable sound system from Antioch. They are meeting in a civic center and have not needed to purchase chairs and tables yet, but they probably will one day. I recommend the plastic 8 ft. tables you can get at office supply or home improvement stores. There are a number of companies that sell furniture to churches, and you can find some good deals online for folding chairs with some fabric padding in the seat and on the back. It is good to have a chair cart as well, one that rolls and will hold at least 50-75 chairs. We also bought round tables to use for special occasions, as well as table carts for both the rectangular and the round tables. You will need some kind of podium to preach from, and we have always preferred a wooden one that is wide enough for a Bible or two and the remote that I use to change the power point slides while I am preaching. You can buy communion equipment from church suppliers. We own the silver trays that are handy for the juice and the bread, and we buy boxes of communion cups (1000 ct.) when needed. Most Christian bookstores keep communion supplies in stock.

There is plenty more to consider when it comes to property and what kind of supplies and equipment you will need, but that's enough to get you started. There is the outside property to consider as well, and a place for children to play and Moms to sit and talk while they supervise. We have just purchased new playground equipment and men in our church will install it. We also have work days at the church twice a year, spring and fall. On these Saturdays, a lot of the deep cleaning and the yard maintenance get done. As the saying goes, "Many hands make light work." We also build relationships as we work together side-by-side.

Chapter Thirteen

How Do We Get the Word Out?

I heard from a friend of mine recently in a city about two hours away. He started a family-integrated church in 2007 and was wondering what to do to market the church. "How do we get the word out, to let people know we even exist?" he asked.

I can think of a lot of things I would *not* do. We have never been interested in holding a dog and pony show on Sunday mornings, and making sure the local media knows about it so we can get press in order to attract people to the church. Something (or Someone) in me militates against that in a powerful way—I think it's the Holy Spirit. We have always resisted the urge to ever start a program or a ministry that has as its primary purpose to draw people in who don't normally attend church, or who attend other churches. The primary purpose of the church, remember, is to glorify the Lord and to equip the saints for the work of ministry, not to try and attract the lost (or the disgruntled) to our church.

I write a weekly newspaper column for the local paper, and the tagline at the end of the column *does* say that I am the pastor of Antioch Community Church in Elon. But the column is not an advertisement for our church. I never write a column to describe what we are doing and to invite people to come. I write the column for two reasons: to disciple the believer and to intrigue the sinner. Perhaps the Lord will then draw the sinner to Himself. But I primarily write with the churched-believer in mind. I also have a one-minute radio spot on a nearby station every weekday afternoon. It is an expense for the church, unlike the column in the newspaper which is published for free and I write for free. The radio spot is designed for the exact same purpose as the column: to disciple the believer and intrigue the sinner. Now, there *have* been occasions when someone has come to Antioch because either they read my column or they heard my radio spot. I can think of one family in particular who recently joined, and they first heard about Antioch through the radio. So, in a sense I guess those two mediums have contributed to "getting the word out."

I also speak almost every year at the North Carolina home school conference. There have been several families who heard me speak there and ended up coming to the church. Or they have heard me speak at homeschool graduations, or their son or daughter has taken my writing or public speaking classes at Veritas, a homeschool co-op that meets at Antioch every Wednesday during the school year. I don't do any of those things to attract people to the church but to serve the homeschool community.

All of that is to say this: by ***far***, the number one way we have "gotten the word out" about Antioch is by word of mouth. One of our members will tell someone else in the community about the church and then…this is the key…they will actually *invite* them to come! **I have heard estimates that range as low as 80% and as high as 98% of the people who attend a church for the first time do so because someone invited them to.** The greatest asset to church growth, besides the power of the Holy Spirit to draw people, is the membership. If your members are excited about what is happening in the church, they will not be able to keep quiet about it. They will talk about the church at the grocery store, at the Little League game, at the homeschool support group meeting, and across the clothesline with their neighbors. That's the best way to get the word out, and it's free.

When I am asked how a family can find others who might be interested in a family-integrated church, I always tell them to talk about it to the people in the local homeschool support group. The same advice goes for a new family-integrated church plant: put flyers up at the homeschool support group meetings. If the support group has an email loop, send an email out to everyone, announcing about your church, where it is, when it meets, and a basic statement of faith that includes the fact that you are a Christ-centered and family-integrated church, in that order! You may also want to give them your church's website in the email.

What? No website?! One of the best ways to serve the entire Christian community in your city, while also getting the word out about your church, is to design a website. It is worth every penny to hire a professional who can design the website that will be attractive, user-friendly, and helpful to all who want to learn more about your church before they ever visit. Times have changed, and the typical person who shows up for the first time at a church these days has already learned all he can about that church on the web. If that is the first impression your church is presenting to the public, you want it to be a good one. Besides the public relations aspect of the website, it will also be a tool for the community. Include articles there that give a good apologetic for the family-integrated church. You may want to have links to other good ministries' websites or information about upcoming conferences that will benefit the family. You also may want to have a blog.

One of the benefits of a blog is that it gives you a way to let people in other areas of the country know about what you are doing. By 'tagging' an entry in the blog with the keywords "family-integrated church," for example, you are providing internet search engines with bait at your site for whoever is out there fishing for information about that subject. If someone in Portland, Oregon 'googles' the words "Family-Integrated Church," one of the links that will come up will be the 'url' for your blog entry where you just wrote about your church and why you worship together as a family. That may not help you, since your church is in North Carolina or Virginia, but hold on… The person in Portland is intrigued by your argument for the family-integrated church, and they have a friend or relative who lives in your city. The next thing you know, that friend is visiting your church because they heard about you from their friend in Oregon. Or, that person in Oregon gets word that he is being transferred to the east coast to…you guessed it…your city. Neither of those scenarios is out of the question; either one *could* happen. At the very least, your blog will be a place where the people in your church can come to discuss and debate the issues of the day and the biblical worldview with which we all need to approach them.

Your website also should have a page that defines who you are and what you believe: a statement of faith, at the very least. Add a constitution and bylaws, if you want to really go all out. When the new elders for Cornerstone Bible Church began to hammer out what was most important to them, they came up with four core values, four legs of the stool, if you will: expository preaching, discipleship, family-integration, and elder-leadership. Those four values can be given as an 'elevator speech' to explain to someone on the way to the 7th floor what their church is all about. Of course, their church is about much more than those four values, and that's why the elders of the new work have also adopted a statement of belief that maps out their biblical convictions about man, sin, the person of Jesus Christ, salvation, and more.

Antioch Community Church has a constitution on our website that begins with the articles of faith (statement of belief). It continues after that with an explanation of how our church is governed. What is expected of the elders and the deacons, how a pastor is selected and compensated, how church discipline is administered, what is expected of the members of the church, and more. There is a good reason to have a constitution that is simply stated and has biblical grounding that is documented for each point: it gives the elders and the members a place of agreement about issues of doctrine or polity. If the constitution is not simply stated, it will create confusion. If it is not biblically grounded, it is not worth the paper it is written on or the space it takes up on the web. If either (confusion or unbiblical doctrine) is present, the enemy will find his way into the church and sow seeds of discord. Every effort must be made by the elders to have the constitution and articles of faith written as clearly and correctly as possible. Even then, you still may find yourselves going back and making changes in it as you go along. For example, we used to have in our constitution that we would have nominations for men to serve as deacons "in the fall of the year." We took that out a while back because we didn't want someone to 'beat us over the head' with our own words. There has been many a fall when we did not have a need for a new deacon or deacons, so we removed that requirement from the constitution. On the other hand, we have *not* had to go back and change anything in our articles of faith! (For your information, I have included our church's Articles of Faith in the appendix. Our complete church constitution can be found on our website, www.antiochchurch.cc Feel free to adapt any or all of it for your own use.)

Newspaper columns, radio spots, word of mouth, websites…

The bottom line on how to get the word out is this: Jesus said, ***I will build My church, and the gates of Hades shall not prevail against it.*** (Matthew 16:18) He also instructed His disciples to ***pray the Lord of the harvest to send out laborers into His harvest.*** (Luke 10:2) I have quoted the first verse thousands of times, reminding myself, the other elders, and the church that He is in charge of our growth. We must be disciplined to have depth, digging into the Word, walking in obedience to what it says, developing a vital prayer life, and loving one another with a fervent love. All of these things will provide depth in our Christian walk. But ultimately only the LORD can provide height. He alone can make a church grow. Only the Lord of the harvest can send out laborers into His harvest. And that is why I have prayed that second verse, Luke 10:2, thousands of times. I prayed it this morning, as I walked through the sanctuary, praying for the church, praying for some of the individual members by name. I also prayed for the members who haven't gotten here yet, asking the Lord to thrust forth His laborers. I often pray that the Lord will bring laborers and servants to Antioch, people who have a hunger and a thirst for God and for His life and for His Word. I also pray that He will keep those away who are divisive, those who are wolves in sheep's clothing, those who come in to devour the flock. Who is in charge of our church 'growth and protection plan?' GOD is!

Chapter Fourteen

What Does it Look Like?

One of the questions I hear the most is, "How do you do it? What does a typical service at a family-integrated church look like?" Well, the truth is, it looks a lot like a service at a program-driven church, probably, except all the children are in there. So…it may not *sound* like a service in a program-driven church, if you catch my drift. It may be a lot noisier. At times.

The last chapter of *Family-Integrated Church* is devoted to answering the question, 'how do we do it?' so let me give you a lengthy excerpt, which I have updated and tweaked:

The worship service begins at 10:00, and we have greeters at the front door with bulletins beginning at 9:45. I will often encourage our greeters (who are typically older teenage girls) to practice hospitality with a big smile as people arrive at the front door. We want all who come on Sunday to see joyful smiles on friendly people who welcome them to the gathering of God's people at Antioch!

The service will usually begin with one of the elders greeting the people from the platform, encouraging them to enter into a place of worship in their hearts. He may read a Scripture passage (just a verse or two, usually) and comment on it as he welcomes the people and invites them into the Lord's presence. He will pray, and then the music team will lead in song.

During the singing, all of the families and singles are worshiping the Lord together. There is no nursery during this time, and babies' squealing blends right in with our voices raised to Him in praise.

After 25-30 minutes of worship singing, the songs will come to a close. The worship leader will pray and then invite people to greet one another. It is during this time that those with babies may take them to a nursery that we offer just during the sermon. Most choose to keep their little ones in the service. As people are greeting, hugging, and just enjoying being together, I am preparing to preach (or someone else is). When it seems good, I will welcome everyone, invite the visitors to fill out a card in the pew-pocket, and I will explain about the nursery and the nursing moms' room. I will then ask everyone to stand in honor of God's Word, and I will read the text for the sermon, as they follow along in their Bibles. Finally, I will pray, leading the people through a few moments of quiet confession. During those few minutes, we are led to a place of asking the Lord to search us and try our hearts, and we take that time to confess our sins to Him, confident He will cleanse us (1 John 1:9). After the prayer, the people will take their seats, and prepare to study the passage with me. In the bulletins each week we include a half sheet of card stock that says "Sermon Title, Date, Speaker, and Passage" on it, and many will use those to take notes. Some have a filing system they use to keep the notes, some keep them in their Bibles, and many children take notes and sometimes draw pictures of what they are hearing in the sermon.

I like to use Power Point with my sermons, because I know that in the congregation every Sunday there are auditory learners *and* visual learners. (There are kinesthetic learners, too, but we can only hope that they will use the bulletin insert and take notes!) The Power Point is normally a simple outline, but on occasion I will include a picture or graphic, if it is helpful. For example, when I preached on 1 Samuel 17, I showed the folks a picture of the Valley of Elah, where David and Goliath actually fought. Well, where *David* fought. Goliath just talked loud and then died!

I will preach for 40-50 minutes, usually, and most of the time I will open it up for questions or testimony immediately after. This has been such a blessing because it gives the people of God an opportunity to hear from Him as He speaks through *anyone* in the congregation that day who has a word that will emphasize or even complete what I have been preaching! There have been many times that someone will add something to what I have just preached that completed the sermon, if you will. Is it intimidating to know that someone may say something that sounds 'better' than what I just said? Sure! But I wouldn't have it any other way. That keeps me humble and it keeps the eyes of the congregation on the Lord, not on a man. It is also intimidating to know that someone may disagree or challenge or even say something unbiblical as a 'testimony.' That has rarely happened, and as I have already written, it is a risk I am willing to take in order to give the people in the church the freedom and the opportunity to hear from the Lord and to encourage the church with what He says to them from His Word.

On rare occasions, I will issue an invitation after I preach for people to respond by coming forward for prayer, as the Lord leads. But the sermon *always* includes an invitation to respond to the Lord in some way, dictated by the text we have looked at that day. If it is the first Sunday of the month, we will take communion together after the sermon and discussion time. I ask different mature men in the congregation to lead the communion so that responsibility is shared.

After the question and answer time (and communion), one of the other men of the church will lead the congregation in a time of "thanksgivings." We have done this since day one at Antioch, and it has always been a time of blessing and encouragement. The brother who is leading has a handheld microphone and will take it to anyone in the congregation who has something to share. The people know this time is coming every Sunday, and so they are usually prepared. We have heard everything from birthday announcements to witnessing stories to a new job to a new baby on the way to a testimony of God's miraculous intervention or healing to something a child said that week that blessed the family. You name it. But it has almost always been something that edifies the body and glorifies the Lord. Very rarely has anyone taken advantage of this opportunity to share something in the flesh or to promote an idea that is not biblical.

At some point during the sharing time, the leader will ask the ushers to come and receive the offering. The ushers can range from fathers to teens to younger boys of 9 or 10 years old.

When the sharing time is over, there will be an opportunity for anyone to give an announcement or a prayer request. This may also be the time that we introduce a new family or single that has gone through the New Members Class and desires to join. Or a family has a new baby they want to have dedicated by the elders. Or we may pray for a brother who is going to Iraq. Or for a family going on a short-term missions trip. Or for someone who is sick and is calling for the elders to anoint with oil and pray, as James 5 teaches. Whatever we are praying for, the elders are there to lead, but anyone in the congregation who wants to join us up front to pray is welcome and invited to do so.

At the end of this ministry time, I will close the service with a prayer, and then I will speak the blessing of Numbers 6:24-26 over the congregation:

> ***The LORD bless you and keep you;***
> ***The LORD make His face shine upon you,***
> ***and be gracious to you;***
> ***The LORD lift up His countenance upon you,***
> ***and give you peace.***

With that, the final AMEN is said and the people are dismissed.

Vance Havner used to say, "Most churches start at 11:00 sharp and end at 12:00 dull."

We start at 10:00. But we never end at 12:00 dull. We end at 11:45 or 12:00 or sometimes even 12:15, but the body of Christ has been sharpened and encouraged in their faith. They usually linger for 20-30 minutes to talk and hug and enjoy the love of the fellowship we have in Christ.

After the service we may have a meal together. We encourage people to bring a covered dish and stay after church for fellowship around the tables. Usually 5-10 families, sometimes more, will stay. Sometimes we encourage everyone to stay for lunch. We may have a special event happening, like a baby shower that everyone is invited to in the fellowship hall as we eat lunch. Or we may have a slide show in the sanctuary after lunch where we get an "end of the year review" of all God did that year through pictures and music. Sometimes we may have a big volleyball game after lunch. But on these Sundays when everyone is encouraged to stay, we usually have 150-180 people who will sit down together and eat. That's a special time to get to know the families or singles that are new or 'new to you!'

That's a snapshot of what it looks like at Antioch. It may look completely different at your church plant. But I hope you will include some form of each component: singing praise to the Lord, hearing the Word preached, communion (whether it's once a month or more often), giving tithes and offerings to the Lord, sharing words of encouragement and testimony with one another, fellowship, and prayer. Sounds a lot like Acts 2:42, doesn't it?

And they continued steadfastly in the apostles' doctrine and fellowship, in the breaking of bread, and in prayers.

Chapter Fifteen

Final Thoughts

I hope this book has been helpful to you, and that I have succeeded in answering at least *most* of your questions about how to plant a family-integrated church. There is more information in the appendix for you, including an excellent article by Tim Keller, pastor of Redeemer Presbyterian Church in New York entitled, "Why Plant Churches." There is also a survey done by Jarrod Michel, a new friend of mine who is doing his master's thesis at Denver Seminary in Littleton, Colorado on the subject of family-integrated churches. It is a very thorough questionnaire, designed to gain an understanding of why a church may want to be family-integrated or want to move in that direction.

I will close this chapter with a column that I wrote for the local newspaper. It was published on the day before Cornerstone Bible Church began in Asheboro, NC, a church plant sent out from Antioch Community Church.

Multiplication is better than addition

OK, I have never been accused of being a math whiz. I have always believed the statistic that says, "5 out of every 3 people are no good in math." I don't understand that statistic, but by grannies I believe it! However, math whiz or no, I cannot be fooled about one thing: multiplication is better than addition.

Think about it. If Johnny has two apples and then Susie gives Johnny another apple, how many would Johnny have now? Well, it depends on whether Johnny is hungry or not. But assuming he exercises a little bit of delayed gratification, Johnny now has three apples. But if Susie *multiplies* Johnny's apples by two, how many would he have now? Go ahead and get a calculator. I'll wait.

That's right! Johnny's two apples turns into four by the power of multiplication. That reminds me of the old question, would you rather have one million dollars now or one penny doubled every day for thirty days? If you take the one million, you don't understand the power of multiplication, because you would be leaving over 4.3 million dollars on the table. Multiplication is amazing.

That's one of the reasons why we believe in it as a fundamental principle of church growth. Tomorrow, five families will leave Antioch Community Church to launch a new work, Cornerstone Bible Church, in Asheboro, NC. We couldn't be more excited about it. We feel like proud new parents, beaming at our new baby, telling all who pass by the nursery, "That's our baby! Isn't she beautiful?" We have long held the view at Antioch that the best way a church can serve a community is not by seeing how big it can get but by following the principles of Scripture that teach church planting. Addition is fine, and there are many who believe in it as a core tenet of church growth. They do everything they can to add people to the church. In the process, sometimes that leads to a dilution of the message: "We don't want to offend, so we will preach what people want to hear." Sometimes that leads to a loss of community: "I don't know anybody here anymore; there are just so many people, I feel like a number." Sometimes that leads to a lack of maturity; Vance Havner used to say that the modern church tends to be a mile wide and an inch deep.

Let me hasten to say that the Lord uses and blesses His church, and none of us have it all right. We have a long way to go and a lot to correct and plenty that we can do better. But we are committed to this idea of church planting and cannot wait to see what happens in Asheboro. We know they will have a healthy start. They are led by two elders, men who are biblically qualified to serve in that role. They are committed to expository preaching and discipleship. They are family-integrated, which means that families will worship together and not be divided at the front door and sent in different directions. They are devoted to Jesus Christ, who said, "I will build my church, and the gates of hell will not prevail against it." (Matthew 16:18)

They are also committed to church planting and believe in the power of multiplication. That's why I wouldn't be surprised if we get word one day that Cornerstone is preparing to send out its first church plant. Because multiplication is better than addition.

May God bless you as you seek the Lord about helping to plant a new church for His glory! If there is anything I can do to help, please feel free to contact me at markfox@antiochchurch.cc. I would love to come and do a workshop or a conference with your group on the family-integrated church, if you desire. Just email me and we will talk about it. Check our church website, also, for conferences we will be holding at Antioch Community Church that are related to the family-integrated church. There is one scheduled for May 1-3, 2009. I would love to see you there!

In Christ,
J. Mark Fox

Appendix 1

Articles of Faith

1. **WE BELIEVE IN THE HOLY SCRIPTURE**: accepting fully the writings of the Old and New Testaments as the inerrant Word of God, verbally inspired in all parts and therefore altogether sufficient as our only infallible and authoritative rule of faith and practice. Psalm 119:160; Proverbs 30:5a; II Timothy 3:16-17; II Peter 1:19-21.
2. **WE BELIEVE IN THE ONE TRUE GOD**: who is an intelligent, sovereign, spiritual and personal Being perfect, infinite, and eternal in His being, holiness and love, wisdom and power; absolutely separate from and above the world as its Creator, yet everywhere present in the world as the Upholder of all things. He is revealed to us as Father, Son, and Holy Spirit, three distinct persons but without division of nature, essence, or being, and each having a distinct ministry in God's relation to His creation and people. Genesis 1:1; Exodus 15:11; Psalm 83:18; Psalm 139:7-9; Matthew 28:19; John 10:30; John 15:26.
3. **WE BELIEVE IN THE LORD JESUS CHRIST**: who is the second Person of the Triune God, the eternal Word and Only Begotten Son; that without any change in His divine Person, He became man by miracle of the Virgin Birth, thus to continue forever as both true God and true Man, one Person with two

natures; that as Man He was tempted in all points as we are, yet without sin; that as the perfect Lamb of God He gave Himself in death upon the cross, bearing there the sin of the world, and suffering its full penalty of divine wrath in our stead; that He arose from the grave in a glorified body; that as our great High Priest He ascended into heaven, there to appear before the face of God as our advocate and Intercessor. John 1:1, 14; John 3:16; Matthew 1:18-25; Galatians 4:4-5; Philippians 2:6-10; I Corinthians 15:3-7; Hebrews 4:14-16; I John 2:1-2.

4. **WE BELIEVE IN THE HOLY SPIRIT**: who is the Third Person of the Trinity; and the living Agent in nature, revelation and redemption; that He convicts the world concerning sin, righteousness and judgment; that He regenerates, indwells, baptizes, seals and anoints all who become children of God through Christ; that He further empowers, guides, teaches, sanctifies and fills believers who daily surrender to Him. John 3:5; John 14:16,17,26; John 16:7-14; Romans 8:9; I Corinthians 12:13; II Corinthians 3:18; Ephesians 1:13; Ephesians 5:18.
5. **WE BELIEVE ALL MEN BY NATURE AND CHOICE SINFUL AND LOST**: that man was the direct creation of God, made in His image and likeness; that by personal disobedience to the revealed will of God, man became a sinful creature, in both nature and practice, thus alienated from the life and family of God, under the righteous judgment and wrath of God, and has within himself no possible means of salvation. Genesis 1:27; Genesis 3:6; Psalm 51:5; Romans 3:23; Romans 5:12, 19; Galatians 3:11.
6. **WE BELIEVE IN SALVATION BY GRACE THROUGH FAITH**: that salvation is the free gift of God, neither merited nor secured in part or in whole

by any virtue or work of man, but received only by personal faith in the Lord Jesus Christ, in whom all true believers have as a present possession the gift of eternal life, a perfect righteousness, sonship in the family of God, deliverance and security from all condemnation, and every spiritual resource needed for life and godliness, and the divine guarantee that they shall never perish; that this salvation affects the whole man; that apart from Christ there is no possible salvation. Ephesians 2:8,9; Titus 3:5; John 1:12; John 3:14; John 10:28,29; Romans 8:1; Philippians 1:6.

7. **WE BELIEVE IN RIGHTEOUS LIVING AND GODLY WORKS**: not as a means of salvation in any sense, but as its proper evidence and fruit; and therefore as Christians we should obey the Word of our Lord, seek the things which are above, walk as he walked, accept as our solemn responsibility the duty and privileges of bearing the Gospel to a lost world; remembering that a victorious and fruitful Christian life is possible only for those who in gratitude for the infinite and undeserved mercies of God have presented themselves wholly to Christ. Ephesians 2:10; Romans 12:1,2; Philippians 2:16.
8. **WE BELIEVE IN THE EXISTENCE OF SATAN**: who originally was created a holy and perfect being, but through pride and wicked ambition rebelled against God, thus becoming utterly depraved in character, the great adversary of God and His people, leader of all other evil angels and wicked spirits, the deceiver and god of this present world: that his powers are vast, but strictly limited by the permissive will of God who overrules all his wicked devices for good; that he was defeated and judged at the cross, and therefore his final doom is certain; that we are able to resist and overcome him only in the armor of

God, by the blood of the Lamb and through the power of the Holy Spirit. Isaiah 14:12-15; Ephesians 6:12; I Peter 5:8; I John 3:8; Revelation 12:9-11; Revelation 20:10.

9. **WE BELIEVE IN OUR LORD'S PERSONAL, IMMINENT RETURN**: for His redeemed ones and His coming in glory to judge the rebellious and to establish His reign on earth. John 14:1-3; I Corinthians 15:51,52; Philippians 3:20; I Thessalonians 1:10; I Thessalonians 4:13-18; Titus 2:11-14; II Thessalonians 2:7-10; Matthew 24:29-31; Zechariah 14:4-11.
10. **WE BELIEVE IN THE ETERNAL LIFE**: and everlasting blessedness of the saved, and the eternal conscious punishment of the lost. John 1:5; Jude 24; Matthew 25:41; Mark 9:42-48; Revelation 20:11-15.
11. **WE BELIEVE IN THE PRIESTHOOD OF ALL BELIEVERS**: that Christ is our Great High Priest and through Him every born-again person has direct access into God's presence without the need of a human priest; that the believer has the right and responsibility to personally study and interpret the Scriptures guided by the Holy Spirit. John 14:6; Hebrews 4:16; II Timothy 2:15; I Peter 2:1,5,9.
12. **WE BELIEVE IN THE LORDSHIP OF JESUS CHRIST**: that He alone is Head of the Body of Christ, into which all true believers are baptized by the Holy Spirit; that all members of this one spiritual body should assemble and identify themselves in local churches. I Corinthians 12:13; Ephesians 1:22,23; Ephesians 4:11-15; Galatians 1:22.
13. **WE BELIEVE IN THE IMPORTANCE OF THE LOCAL CHURCH**: that a Christian church is a local assembly of born-again baptized believers united

in organization to practice the ordinance, to meet together for worship, prayer, fellowship, teaching and a united testimony, and to actively engage in carrying out the Great Commission. Acts 2:41-42; I Corinthians 11:2; Matthew 28:19-20.

14. **WE BELIEVE IN THE INDEPENDENCE AND AUTONOMY OF THE LOCAL CHURCH**: that each Christian church is free to govern itself without ecclesiastical interference, and should cooperate with other Christian churches as the Holy Spirit leads, that it is responsible to follow the pattern of the Christian church and is directly accountable to God. Matthew 18:17; Acts 6:1-5; Acts 13:1-3; Acts 15:22-23.
15. **WE BELIEVE THE ORDINANCES GIVEN TO THE LOCAL CHURCH ARE TWO, BAPTISM AND THE LORD'S SUPPER**: that baptism is by immersion of believers in water, thus portraying the death, burial and the resurrection of Jesus Christ; that the Lord's Supper is the partaking of the bread and cup by the believer as a continuing memorial of the broken body and shed blood of Christ. Matthew 28:19-20; Acts 2:41; Acts 8:38-39; Matthew 26:26-30; I Corinthians 11:23-34.

Appendix 2

Dealing With Money

What about money? Set up a bank account with a local bank that you trust, under the name of the church. We have ours set up so that two different men can sign checks, just in case we need a check on a Sunday that the normal check-signer is not there. But we have not set it up to require both signatures. We just have not believed that to be necessary. I recommend you have two men who share the responsibility for taking care of the funds, one taking care of income, one taking care of outgo. One man should count the offering, deposit it, and keep records of who gave what each week for the end of the year tax receipts. If you believe it is good to have two men count the offering, for accountability purposes, that is fine. We have never believed that to be necessary and have never had a problem with it. The second man is responsible for writing the checks and paying the bills. He gets the deposit slip from the income man, keeps records of what we have in the bank, and writes the checks each month (on time!) to pay the bills, the salaries, and the missions giving. Once a month, the outgo man will give a report to the elders and deacons (we meet collectively on the first Sunday of every month; the deacons do not meet as a separate entity). The report will include the income for the previous month and the line by line expenditures, as well as the year-to-date totals.

What about insurance? I recommend the church have a good policy to cover their possessions (whether they own their building and property or not). This will protect against fire, floods, theft and vandalism. I also recommend the church purchase a liability policy to protect the elders and any staff members against law suits. If a grieved member decides to retaliate for counseling he received from the pastor or a member hurts himself walking to his car in the parking lot, the church should be covered against damaging lawsuits. I know what 1 Corinthians 6 says…but it just takes one person in the church who does not know or who does not care to ruin the church financially.

What about incorporation? We have never felt that it was necessary at Antioch. We are a tax-exempt organization under the laws of North Carolina because we are a church, and have not jumped through the hoops to become a 501-C3. There are arguments on either side of this issue that make sense, so it is something you need to decide for yourself. Whether you incorporate or not, you DO need a federal Tax-ID (or EIN) number. Go to www.irs.gov to find information on how to apply for that.

Appendix 3

WHY PLANT CHURCHES

Tim Keller
Redeemer Presbyterian Church
Feb. 2002

Introduction

The vigorous, continual planting of new congregations is the single most crucial strategy for 1) the numerical growth of the Body of Christ in any city, and 2) the continual corporate renewal and revival of the existing churches in a city. Nothing else—not crusades, outreach programs, para-church ministries, growing mega-churches, congregational consulting, nor church renewal processes—will have the consistent impact of dynamic, extensive church planting. This is an eyebrow raising statement. But to those who have done any study at all, it is not even controversial.

The normal response to discussions about church planting is something like this:

A. 'We already have plenty of churches that have lots and lots of room for all the new people who have come to the area. Let's get *them* filled before we go off building any new ones.'

B. 'Every church in this community used to be more full than it is now. The churchgoing public is a 'shrinking pie'. A new church here will just take people from churches already hurting and weaken everyone.'

C. 'Help the churches that are struggling first. A new church doesn't help the ones we have that are just keeping their nose above water. We need *better* churches, not more churches.'

These statements appear to be 'common sense' to many people, but they rest on several wrong assumptions. The error of this thinking will become clear if we ask *'Why is church planting so crucially important?'* Because—

A. We want to be true to THE BIBLICAL MANDATE

1. Jesus' essential call was to plant churches. Virtually all the great evangelistic challenges of the New Testament are basically calls to plant churches, not simply to share the faith. The 'Great Commission' (Matt.28: 18-20) is not just a call to *'make disciples'* but to *'baptize'*. In Acts and elsewhere, it is clear that baptism means incorporation into a worshipping community with accountability and boundaries (cf. Acts 2:41-47). The only way to be truly sure you are increasing the number of Christians in a town is to increase the number of churches. Why? Much traditional evangelism aims to get a 'decision' for Christ. Experience, however, shows us that many of these 'decisions' disappear and never result in changed lives. Why? Many, many decisions are not really conversions, but often only the beginning of a journey of seeking God. (Other decisions are very definitely the moment of a 'new birth', but this differs from person to person.) Only a person who is being 'evangelized' in the context of an on-going worshipping and shepherding community can be sure of finally coming home into vital, saving faith. This is why a leading missiologist like C. Peter Wagner can say, *"Planting* *new churches is the most effective evangelistic methodology known under heaven."*[1]

2. Paul's whole strategy was to plant urban churches. The greatest missionary in history, St. Paul, had a rather simple, two-fold strategy. First, he went into the largest city of the region (cf. Acts 16:9,12), and second, he planted churches in each city (cf. Titus 1:5- *"appoint elders in every town"*). Once Paul had done that, he could say that he had *'fully preached'* the gospel in a region and that he had *'no more work'* to do there (cf. Romans 15:19,23). This means Paul had two controlling assumptions: a) that the way to most permanently influence a country was through its chief cities, and b) the way to most permanently influence a city was to plant churches in it. Once he had accomplished this in a city, he moved on. He knew that the rest that needed to happen would follow.

Response: *'But,'* many people say, *'that was in the beginning. Now the country (at least* <u>*our*</u> *country) is filled with churches. Why is church planting important* <u>*now*</u>*?"* We also plant churches because—

B. We want to be true to THE GREAT COMMISSION. Some facts—

1. New churches best reach a) new generations, b) new residents, and c) new people groups. First (a) younger adults have always been disproportionately found in newer congregations. Long-established congregations develop traditions (such as time of worship, length of service, emotional responsiveness, sermon topics, leadership-style, emotional atmosphere, and thousands of other tiny customs and mores), which reflect the sensibilities of long-time leaders from the older generations who have the influence and money to control the church life.

This does not reach younger generations. Second, (b) new residents are almost always reached better by new congregations. In older congregations, it may require tenure of 10 years before you are allowed into places of leadership and influence, but in a new church, new residents tend to have equal power with long-time area residents.

Last, (c) new socio-cultural groups in a community are always reached better by new congregations. For example, if new white-collar commuters move into an area where the older residents were farmers, it is likely that a new church will be more receptive to the myriad of needs of the new residents, while the older churches will continue to be oriented to the original social group. And new racial groups in a community are best reached by a new church that is intentionally multi-ethnic from the start. For example: if an all-Anglo neighborhood becomes 33% Hispanic, a new, deliberately bi-racial church will be far more likely to create 'cultural space' for newcomers than will an older church in town. Finally, brand new immigrant groups nearly always can only be reached by churches ministering in their own language. If we wait until a new group is assimilated into American culture enough to come to our church, we will wait for years without reaching out to them.

[Note: Often, a new congregation for a new people-group can be planted *within* the overall structure of an existing church. It may be a new Sunday service at another time, or a new network of house churches that are connected to a larger, already existing congregation. Nevertheless, though it may technically not be a new independent congregation, it serves the same function.]

In summary, new congregations *empower* new people and new peoples much more quickly and readily than can older churches. Thus they always have and always will reach them with greater facility than long-established bodies. This means, of course, that church planting is not only for 'frontier regions' or 'pagan' countries that we are trying to see *become* Christian. Christian countries will have to maintain vigorous, extensive church planting simply to *stay* Christian!

2. New churches best reach the unchurched—period. Dozens of denominational studies have confirmed that the average new church gains most of its new members (60-80%) from the ranks of people who are not attending any worshipping body, while churches over 10-15 years of age gain 80-90% of new members by transfer from other congregations.[2] This means that the average new congregation will bring 6-8 times more new people into the life of the Body of Christ than an older congregation of the same size.

So though established congregations provide many things that newer churches often cannot, older churches in general will never be able to match the effectiveness of new bodies in reaching people for the kingdom. Why would this be? As a congregation ages, powerful internal institutional pressures lead it to allocate most of its resources and energy toward the concerns of its members and constituents, rather than toward those outside its walls. This is natural and to a great degree desirable. Older congregations therefore have a stability and steadiness that many people thrive on and need. This does not mean that established churches cannot win new people. In fact, many non-Christians will only be reached by churches with long roots in the community and the trappings of stability and respectability.

However, new congregations, in general, are forced to focus on the needs of its *non*-members, simply in order to get off the ground. So many of its leaders have come very recently from the ranks of the un-churched, that the congregation is far more sensitive to the concerns of the non-believer. Also, in the first two years of our Christian walk, we have far more close, face-to-face relationships with non-Christians than we do later. Thus a congregation filled with people fresh from the ranks of the un-churched will have the power to invite and attract many more non-believers into the events and life of the church than will the members of the typical established body.

What does this mean practically? If we want to reach our city—should we try to renew older congregations to make them more evangelistic, or should we plant lots of new churches? But that question is surely a false either-or dichotomy. We should do both! Nevertheless, all we have been saying proves that, despite the occasional exceptions, the only wide scale way to bring in lots of new Christians to the Body of Christ in a permanent way is to plant new churches.

To throw this into relief, imagine Town-A and Town-B and Town-C are the same size, and they each have 100 churches of 100 persons each. But in Town-A, all the churches are over 15 years old, and then the overall number of active Christian churchgoers in that town will be shrinking, even if four or five of the churches get very 'hot' and double in attendance. In Town-B, 5 of the churches are under 15 years old, and they along with several older congregations are winning new people to Christ, but this only offsets the normal declines of the older churches. Thus the overall number of active Christian churchgoers in that town will be staying the same. Finally, in Town-C, 30 of the churches are under 15 years old. In this town, the overall number of active Christian churchgoers will be on a path to grow 50% in a generation.[3]

Response: *'But,'* many people say, *'what about all the existing churches that need help? You seem to be ignoring them.'* Not at all. We also plant churches because—

C. We want to continually RENEW THE WHOLE BODY OF CHRIST.

It is a great mistake to think that we have to choose *between* church planting and church renewal. Strange as it may seem, the planting of new churches in a city is one of the very best ways to revitalize many older churches in the vicinity and renew the whole Body of Christ. Why?

1. First, the new churches bring new ideas to the whole Body. There is plenty of resistance to the idea that we need to plant new churches to reach the constant stream of 'new' groups and generations and residents. Many congregations insist that all available resources should be used to find ways of helping existing churches reach them. However, there is no better way to teach older congregations about new skills and methods for reaching new people groups than by planting new churches. It is the new churches that will have freedom to be innovative and they become the 'Research and Development' department for the whole Body in the city. Often the older congregations were too timid to try a particular approach or were absolutely sure it would 'not work here'. But when the new church in town succeeds wildly with some new method, the other churches eventually take notice and get the courage to try it themselves.

2. Second, new churches are one of the best ways to surface creative, strong leaders for the whole Body. In older congregations, leaders emphasize tradition, tenure, routine, and kinship ties. New congregations, on the other hand, attract a higher percentage of venturesome people who value creativity, risk, innovation and future orientation. Many of these men and women would never be attracted or compelled into significant ministry apart from the appearance of these new bodies. Often older churches 'box out' many people with strong leadership skills who cannot work in more traditional settings. New churches thus attract and harness many people in the city whose gifts would otherwise not be utilized in the work of the Body. These new leaders benefit the whole city-Body eventually.

3. Third, the new churches challenge other churches to self-examination. The "success" of new churches often challenges older congregations in general to evaluate themselves in substantial ways. Sometimes it is only in contrast with a new church that older churches can finally define their *own* vision, specialties, and identity. Often the growth of the new congregation gives the older churches hope that 'it can be done', and may even bring about humility and repentance for defeatist and pessimistic attitudes. Sometimes, new congregations can partner with older churches to mount ministries that neither could do by themselves.

4. Fourth, the new church may be an 'evangelistic feeder' for a whole community. The new church often produces many converts who end up in older churches for a variety of reasons. Sometimes the new church is very exciting and outward facing but is also very unstable or immature in its leadership. Thus some converts cannot stand the tumultuous changes that regularly come through the new church and they move to an existing church. Sometimes the new church reaches a person for Christ, but the new convert quickly discovers that he or she does not 'fit' the socio-economic make up of the new congregation, and gravitates to an established congregation where the customs and culture feels more familiar. Ordinarily, the new churches of a city produce new people not only for themselves, but for the older bodies as well.

Sum: Vigorous church planting is one of the best ways to *renew* the existing churches of a city, as well as the best single way to *grow* the whole Body of Christ in a city.

There is one more reason why it is good for the existing churches of the region to initiate or at least support the planting of churches in a given area. We plant churches—

D. As an exercise in KINGDOM-MINDEDNESS

All in all, church planting helps an existing church the best when the new congregation is voluntarily 'birthed' by an older 'mother' congregation. Often the excitement and new leaders and new ministries and additional members and income 'washes back' into the mother church in various ways and strengthens and renews it. Though there is some pain in seeing good friends and some leaders go away to form a new church, the mother church usually experiences a surge of high self-esteem and an influx of new enthusiastic leaders and members.

However, a new church in the community usually confronts churches with a major issue—the issue of 'kingdom-mindedness'. New churches, as we have seen, draw most of their new members (up to 80%) from the ranks of the unchurched, but they *will* always attract some people out of existing churches. That is inevitable. At this point, the existing churches, in a sense, have a question posed to them: "Are we going to rejoice in the 80%—the new people that the kingdom has gained through this new church, or are we going to bemoan and resent the three families we lost to it?" In other words, our attitude to new church development is a test of whether our mindset is geared to our own institutional turf, or to the overall health and prosperity of the kingdom of God in the city.

Any church that is more upset by their own small losses rather than the kingdoms large gains is betraying its narrow interests. Yet, as we have seen, the benefits of new church planting to older congregations is very great, even if that may not be obvious initially.

SUMMARY

If we briefly glance at the objections to church planting in the introduction, we can now see the false premises beneath the statements. **A.** Assumes that older congregations can reach newcomers as well as new congregations. But to reach new generations and people groups will require *both* renewed older churches and lots of new churches. **B.** Assumes that new congregations will only reach current active churchgoers. But new churches do far better at reaching the unchurched, and thus they are the only way to *increase* the 'churchgoing pie'. **C.** Assumes that new church planting will only discourage older churches. There is a prospect of this, but new churches for a variety of ways, are one of the best ways to renew and revitalize older churches. **D.** Assumes that new churches only work where the population is growing. Actually, they reach people wherever the population is *changing*. If new people are coming in to replace former residents, or new groups of people are coming in—even though the net pop figure is stagnant—new churches are needed.

New church planting is the only way that we can be sure we are going to increase the number of believers in a city and one of the best ways to renew the whole Body of Christ. The evidence for this statement is strong—Biblically, sociologically, and historically. In the end, a lack of kingdom-mindedness may simply blind us to all this evidence. We must beware of that.

APPENDIX A-

HISTORICAL LESSONS

If all this is true, there should be lots of evidence for these principles in church history—and there is.

In 1820, there was one Christian church for every 875 U.S. residents. But from 1860-1906, U.S. Protestant churches planted one new church for increase of 350 in the population, bringing the ratio by the start of WWI to just 1 church for every 430 persons. In 1906 over a third of all the congregations in the country were less than 25 years old.[4] As a result, the percentage of the U.S. population involved in the life of the church rose steadily. For example, in 1776, 17% of the U.S. population was 'religious adherents', but that rose to 53% by 1916.[5]

However, after WWI, especially among mainline Protestants, church planting plummeted, for a variety of reasons. One of the main reasons was the issue of 'turf'. Once the continental U.S. was covered by towns and settlements and churches and church buildings in each one, there was strong resistance from older churches to any new churches being planted in 'our neighborhood'. As we have seen above, new churches are commonly very effective at reaching new people and growing for its first couple of decades. But the vast majority of U.S. congregations reaches their peak in size during the first two or three decades of their existence and then remain on a plateau or slowly shrink.[6] This is due to the factors mentioned above. They cannot assimilate well new people or groups of people as well as new churches. However, older churches have feared the competition from new churches. Mainline church congregations, with their centralized government, were the most effective in blocking new church development in their towns. As a result, however, the mainline churches have shrunk remarkably in the last 20-30 years.[7]

What are the historical lessons? Church attendance and adherence overall in the United States is in decline and decreasing. This cannot be reversed in any other way than in the way it originally had been so remarkably *increasing*. We must plant churches at such a rate that the number of churches per 1,000 population begins to grow again, rather than decline, as it has since WWI.

Notes

[1] C.Peter Wagner, Strategies for Growth (Glendale: Regal, 1987), p. 168.

[2] Lyle Schaller, quoted in D. McGavran and G. Hunter, Church Growth: Strategies that Work (Nashville: Abingdon, 1980), p. 100. See C. Kirk Hadaway, New Churches and Church Growth in the Southern Baptist Convention (Nashville: Broadman, 1987).

[3] See Lyle Schaller, 44 Questions for Church Planters (Nashville: Abingdon, 1991), p.12. Schaller talks about 'The 1% Rule'. Each year any association of churches should plant new congregations at the rate of 1% of their existing total—otherwise, that association will be in decline. That is just 'maintenance'. If an association wants to grow 50%+, it must plant 2-3% per year.

[4] *Ibid*, pp.14-26.

[5] Roger Finke and Rodney Stark, The Churching of America 1776-1990 (New Brunswick: Rutgers, 1992) p.16.

[6] Schaller, 44 Questions, p.23.

[7] See Schaller's case that it is a lack of church planting that is one major cause of the decline of mainline Protestantism. *Ibid*, p.24-26. Finke and

Stark show how independent churches, such as the Baptists, who have had freedom to plant churches without interference, have proliferated their numbers. *Churching*, p.248.

Appendix 4

In conjunction with a Thesis Study
at Denver Seminary in Littleton, Colorado…

Survey of Household and Family-Integrated Churches

Survey Contact: Jarrod Michel

As I define in my Thesis, *Household Approach to Ministry* is the term given to the vision whereby a church moves away from the widely-accepted age-segregated *design* of ministry – and rather – incorporates children, youth, and adults *together* into most areas of church life (including worship, education, and outreach).

This *vision* is the primary subject in the survey below.

Your church was selected to be a part of this survey because it was determined from a cursory review or by referral that your church holds to, or desires to move in the direction of, just such a vision for ministry.

I have noted that while many churches may agree with the *Household Approach to Ministry*, they may use one of several different terms to describe their church. These terms may include: family-integrated, family church, multi-generational, inter-generational, age-integrated, household(s), etc. Perhaps your church uses a different term altogether to describe itself. You will have a chance within this survey to describe your church in your own terms.

The purpose of this survey is to gain an understanding of how your church operates and the purposes behind the vision in which you conduct your ministry. Some taking this survey may have churches fully engaged in this vision, while others may be moving toward the vision, or simply contemplating a move in that direction. Please answer the survey questions below to the best of your ability, given your current circumstances. Please feel free to expand in any area that you feel necessary. Some questions may not be applicable to your church at this time. If you are considering a move in the direction of the vision mentioned above, some of the questions will require that you provide answers based on your *anticipation of ministry* within that new context. At the same time, feel free to point out any concerns that you may have towards this vision of ministry.

I ask that you be candid and truthful in your answers, and without exaggeration. The point of the survey is not to *compare* one church over another, or for you to feel that you are being compared to others (because you are not). My hope is to gain an understanding of what churches are doing as they move to a different understanding of how church and ministry should and/or should not be done. Your answers will be valuable to others considering the value of this spreading vision.

Lastly, the information you provide will help to add to my understanding, and ultimately, the understanding of the readers, Denver Seminary, and other academic institutions that may take note of this thesis upon its completion.

I am extremely grateful to you for taking the time to answer my survey and allowing myself and my professors to see into your heart, and the heart of your church. Thank you.

In Him, Jarrod Michel

Church Name: Antioch Community Church

Mailing Address: P.O. Box 40 Elon, NC 27244

PASTORAL INFORMATION

Pastor's Name: J. Mark Fox

Pastor's Age: 50

Educational Background of the Pastor (describe the highest formal education obtained, including degrees obtained and schools attended). MDiv, Pastoral Ministry, Luther Rice Seminary; M.A., Speech Communication, University of North Carolina – Chapel Hill

What is the primary role of the position of pastor in your church? To lead, feed, protect, and care for the flock, along with the other elders.

Do you meet with other pastors in your community on any kind of regular basis? Yes, once a month, for prayer and lunch.

Please name some theologians, educators, pastors and/or Parachurch ministries that you would consider to be your role models specific to ministry in general, and also with respect to your family-integrated vision. John Piper, Mark Dever, Albert Moehler, Alistair Begg, Alexander Strauch

CHURCH INFORMATION

In what year was your church founded? 1987
Was the church founded by the current pastor? yes

Does your church have a denominational affiliation? If so, with whom? No.

What term do you use to describe your church? (Underline)

> **Family-integrated**, multi-generational, age-integrated, inter-generational, family church, household, or other. *If other, please state briefly.*

Why did you choose the term you did?
I heard the term expressed by Doug Phillips at a conference in 2004 (or somewhere around there) and realized it described what we are at Antioch. We worship together as families.

Would you consider any of the other terms above as also appropriate in describing your church? If so, which ones (or please add others if not listed). I like multi-generational as well.

How do you define the term "family-integrated"? The family is kept together and encouraged to function together as a family at church and outside the church. We do not divide the family into its various age groups when they walk into the front door of the church.

How do you define the term "Household"? A household is made up of a set of parents, one man and one woman, and their children, and any others who may be living with them at the time (like a mother-in-law, e.g.), or it is a single person living alone, or a widow, or a single mom (or dad) and children, etc.

Please describe in brief detail your church's journey towards this approach to ministry (or how you have come to consider this model if you are not active in it yet). We began to put programs on the back burner when we met on a college campus for 9 years for our Sunday morning service. Our mission (to reach the campus with the Gospel) did not really allow for an age-segregated approach to ministry on Sunday morning, and we realized that this (family-integrated) was a healthier way for us to worship and a better way for us to function as a church.

CHURCH GOVERNMENT

Describe your church government (and please include the organization of leaders, i.e. plurality of elders, deacons, other staff, etc.)? We are elder-led. There is a plurality of elders (four of us). There are also four deacons who serve the church.

Are all the leaders of your church understanding of and committed to this vision for ministry? Please elaborate if possible. Yes, very much so.

CHURCH MEMBERSHIP

How many households currently attend on a regular basis (households describes families, singles, widows, those married without children, empty-nesters, etc.)?
67 or 68

Approximately how many adults and children make up your church membership?

Adults 125Children____150____

Please fill in the approximate number of members/participants by age range:

103______Age 12 and under 40____Age 13 to 18

11_Age 19-25 60____Age 25-40

55_Age 40-60 7_____Over age 60

Do you have any single-parent families in your membership? Yes

Do you have any widows in your membership? Yes

Approximately what percentage of your member families:

5__Have their children in public school

___ Have their children in private (or charter) school

95_ Home-school

CHURCH SERVICE (WORSHIP)

Does your church fellowship typically meet every week? Yes

Approximately how long is your typical worship gathering from beginning to end? 2 hours

Please describe a typical church day gathering (i.e. education hour followed by worship followed by fellowship, etc.). 7:30am, elders meet; 9:00am, worship team practices; 9am class (seasonal; not all the time) on different topics, open to all ages; 10am worship service (until noon, usually); fellowship following service

Does your church family regularly share meals as part of its worship day? If so, how often? Yes, every week there are at least 5 or 6 families eating together. Once a quarter or so, we will all meet together for lunch after the service.

Describe briefly your general style of worship? Blended. (Usually 25-30 minutes of singing; mostly contemporary worship songs, with one or two hymns)

If music is a part of your worship service, what styles do you use (psalms, hymns, contemporary music, a capella, musical instruments, etc.)? As above…we have a piano, electric bass, acoustic and electric guitar, congas, violins, flute…

Approximately how long is your average sermon message? 40-50 minutes

Please describe how you draw the children into the message being delivered. I sometimes will ask them to draw me a picture of what I am preaching about. I encourage them to listen, to take notes, etc.

Many in modern churches are concerned about the "noise factor" when keeping infants and small children with parents throughout worship. How does your church handle this? We encourage parents to respect those around them and if their child becomes disruptive to take him out and calm him and bring him back in. But we encourage everyone to give grace and listen carefully! ☺ (We always tell the visitors, especially if they don't have small children, that they will hear better near the front.)

What advice would you give those who struggle with this concern? That it is a learning period that every family who wants to worship as a family has to go through, and we can help each other through this period with encouragement and prayer!

How often does your church celebrate communion? Once a month.

Do all of the children participate in communion alongside their parents? If not, at what point do they begin to participate? Only those who are believers.

When baptisms are held, who baptizes, the Pastor or the parent? One of the elders and the father (if he is present) will baptize.

Does your church baptize infants? No.

Please provide some specifics with respect to how the gospel message is taught and shared to the members of your church, and how the gospel message is provided to those outside of your church. Not sure what you are asking here, but we share the gospel message regularly that every person is a sinner from birth, needs to repent and trust Christ for salvation, and salvation is by grace through faith.

Do you agree with the following statement? A Household Approach to Ministry (or family-integrated church) adds to the effectiveness of living out/spreading of the gospel. If so, please describe. Yes, I think one of the most compelling pictures of the gospel at work transforming lives is a healthy, biblical family. Marriage, also, as Paul said in Eph. 5, is supposed to be a living picture of the relationship between Christ and His church.

CHURCH PROGRAMS AND MINISTRIES

Do you offer age-segregated "Sunday School"? No.

Do you maintain any age-segregated programs (i.e. youth, children, men, women, singles, etc.)? If so, please list. Not age-segregated, no. But the men meet together (all ages, from 12 up) for breakfast once a month, for a retreat once a year (the women do an annual retreat as well). There is a community Bible Study for those in college or older (meets bi-weekly).

Do you maintain any regular equipping programs (i.e. small groups, missions, evangelism, etc.)? If so, please list. Small groups meet weekly in homes. We have mission trips annually, and invite mission speakers in regularly. We do house to house evangelism in the community on occasion.

Do you actively incorporate singles, widows, young-marrieds, young adults, "single teens", into the worship and ministry of the church? If so, please describe how you accomplish that. We encourage anyone to share a testimony or a word of encouragement during the open sharing time every Sunday. The teens help with the worship team, help run the sound board, and do other acts of service. The young boys (ages 9-12) will often take the offering up. We invite the singles and widows to home groups, and to all functions of the church.

Do you offer youth group? No.

If youth group is offered, please state to what degree the parents are involved with their children during the activities/functions.

A. Parent(s) are always with their children.
B. Parent(s) are sometimes with their children.
C. Parent(s) are rarely with their children.

If applicable, please describe the role(s) that parents play in your youth group (i.e. leaders, supporting role, participants, etc.)

What activities/functions does your church promote outside of Sunday? Home groups (mid-week), and other (more-sporadic) ministry opportunities.

Is evangelism an active part of your church? If so, please describe some ways in which evangelism is carried out. Not as a program. I will regularly encourage people to share their faith, especially as it is incorporated in the passage I am preaching from that day. We encourage the home groups to invite family, friends, or neighbors to come to their homes (those who are not saved or not churched).

Please explain mission or evangelical work that your church and/or some of your families have been involved in where families have worked/served together as families. Working at the homeless shelter/soup kitchen; door to door evangelism in the community; having people in our homes for a meal and sharing the gospel.

Have you ever taught on the ministry of Hospitality? Yes.

Do you believe that the family-integrated design of church ministry creates an atmosphere where the church could more easily become inward focused compared to those churches with more traditional age-segregated models of ministry? Please explain. Yes. We have to work on lifting up our eyes to see the fields that are white unto harvest, as Jesus said. An FIC might tend to be inward-focused if family is the goal rather than serving Christ as Lord.

What methods/actions do you incorporate to help prevent your church from becoming in-grown? By in-grown, I mean that the church loses sight of others outside the church and becomes focused primarily on the up-keep of the church and its own members. Preaching often challenges the flock to serve and to reach the lost; we will go into the community door to door as stated above; we will hear testimonies regularly on Sundays from someone in the church who witnessed that week at work or in the marketplace, etc.

FAMILY

Please describe your teaching of the roles for men and women in their families and the church? Please explain how these roles are carried out in your church? We take 1 Cor. 11:3 to be literal truth: man is the head of the family.

Wives are called by God to be helpmeets to their husbands. In the church, men are called to lead. Women can use their gifts and are certainly equal to men in salvation and position with Christ, but they have not been given the role of leadership in the church. We encourage the Titus 2 model of older women teaching younger women about loving their husbands and their children. We encourage the men to take up their responsibilities and lead their families. We do this through expositional preaching (it came up as we worked through Ephesians for 1 and ½ years, we do it through men's breakfasts and retreats, we do it through one on one fellowship and encouragement, we do it through accountability groups that meet weekly for breakfast, etc.

If your church emphasizes fatherly leadership in the individual homes, what changes have you observed in the marriage relationships of the families involved? It has greatly strengthened marriage bonds, given the wives much encouragement and hope, given the men confidence that they *can* lead, and much more.

How has an emphasis on fatherly or Head of Household leadership impacted the relationships between parents and their young children (under 12)? I believe it has caused the children to look at their fathers with more respect and to see him as the spiritual authority in the home. They also start to develop (the boys) a desire to be a spiritual leader like their dads.

How has an emphasis on fatherly or Head of Household leadership impacted the relationships between parents and their teenaged or young adult children (13 to 21)? Same as above, and at this age, the young men really begin to want to model their spiritual behavior after their Dads, if they respect him. If he is leading, firmly but lovingly, then there is a much greater chance that they *will* respect him.

How has a Household Approach to Ministry affected intergenerational relationships between families? (i.e. children with other's parents, parents with other parents, parents with other's children, grandparents with other parents, etc.) I believe it works the same way as above. The children in the church see other adults (most of the time!) as authority figures who deserve their respect and honor. The parents in the church relate well to one another, in part because there is a mutual respect for the job we are all trying to do as parents in our own homes.

Who is responsible for the spiritual nurture of children? The church? The home? Both? Please briefly explain your response. The home is primarily responsible. This is biblical (Deut. 6, Proverbs, Ephesians 6, etc)

Is it a particular focus of your church to place and develop the parents and the home as the primary place where faith is nurtured? Yes.

If a particular focus of your church is to develop the parents into the primary nurturers of their children's spiritual growth, please describe the achievement of that goal when considering the majority of your church members:

A - making progress, but met with some apprehension on the part of the parents;

B - there is a disconnect between what the parents agree they should do and what seems to be occurring in reality;

C - there are some parents who do not like being pressured to become the primary spiritual caretakers of their children;

D – many parents in the church do not feel qualified to lead their children and continue to place primary responsibility for the spiritual growth with the church

E – for the most part, we are seeing the parents accept their role as the primary spiritual caretakers of their children

For the next three questions, please note the following: In using the term Head of Household, *the understanding is that there are occasions where women may be the spiritual leaders of the children in the family, where the fathers are not in a position to take, or do not accept, that role.* Head of Household *would also most certainly include widows, single mothers, etc.*

If a particular focus of your church is to develop the men (or Head of Household) into the role of primary spiritual leader in their home, please describe the achievement of that goal when considering the majority of the fathers, husbands, and Heads of Household in your church:*

A - making progress, but met with some apprehension
B - there is a disconnect between what they agree they should do and what seems to be occurring in reality;
C - there are some who do not like being pressured to become the spiritual leaders of their families;
D – many in the church do not feel qualified to lead their families spiritually
E – for the most part, we are seeing them accept their role as spiritual leader in the home

Please explain how your church leaders equip and/or train the Heads of Household in their role as spiritual leaders of their homes. As has been stated above, through expositional preaching, through home groups (the men share the leadership of these), through men's breakfasts, through retreats, through accountability groups, through one on one discipleship, and sometimes through church discipline!

Does your church include the "non-traditional" Heads of Household (i.e. widows, divorced/single mothers, etc.) in the training sessions specific to Heads of Household? If not, how do you equip them to be the spiritual leaders of their home? No. There are very few non-traditional heads, but we help these on a case by case basis, as needed. The women are very much involved in helping these ladies as well.

Do you believe that a focus on the family can become such a focus of a church that it becomes, in essence, idolatry? If so, then please explain at what point you believe family would become an idol. Yes, I believe that would be the case if a man put his family, his marriage, his children, whatever ahead of his relationship with Christ!

HOUSEHOLD APPROACH TO MINISTRY

What is your primary reason for working within, moving towards, or contemplating this model of church and ministry? Because we believe the Bible teaches it.

Do you consider your move towards (or belief in) this model of ministry based more out of conviction or necessity? (i.e. Some churches may be "multigenerational" simply because they have a relatively small number of people within the congregation.) Please explain briefly. Conviction. The Bible teaches it, *and* we have a 15 year history (since we changed to family-integrated in 1993) of seeing the fruit of this model. It works.

Please state briefly what doctrines/theology you believe are foundational to the household approach to ministry? The headship of man in the home and church. The permanence of marriage. The submission of children to their parents immediately, completely, and joyfully.

If you moved to family-integrated ministry from the traditional age-segregated method and designs, what was the greatest challenge in making that move? Leaving behind some of the 'programs' that some people had come to the church because we had them. It was a lack of trust on our part, but we were afraid we would lose people. We did. But God replaced them. ☺

When considering the integration of this vision with your church ministry, please describe in brief detail some of your successes. Stronger marriages, happier and healthier (spiritually) men and women, greater desire to advance God's Kingdom as a family, bolder communication of the Gospel to those outside the church (people are excited to invite people to Antioch because they know it is a healthy church), more spiritually mature children and teens, quicker maturity of teens into young adults.

When considering the integration of this vision to your church ministry, please describe in brief detail some of your challenges and failures. Just because you don't have a youth group does not mean that a youth culture cannot develop. We have had to deal with that challenge a few times, but God has given grace.

What do you see as the greatest obstacle to overcome when establishing this vision for family-integrated worship, education and ministries? Dealing with people's expectations right up front. Trying to help people understand the biblical call for this model and helping them to buy into it. If they don't, or if they pretend they do, it can be disastrous for the church down the road.

What has been the single greatest challenge to your family-integrated vision? As I said above, dealing with people's expectations in the beginning stages.

What to this day, continues to be the most challenging aspect of the family-integrated design of worship, education and ministries? Not sure there is a great challenge now. We do have to explain ourselves to those in other churches a lot, but that's an opportunity!

What has been the greatest blessing? The transformation of the men into spiritual leaders.

When you think of the "vision-splendor" of when you began your ministry, how has that vision changed after some time "in the trenches"? (i.e. Are your attitudes the same? What was realistic or unrealistic? Were there any aspects of this approach that were a greater success than you anticipated? Were there theories of ministry application that did not work out so well? What caught you by surprise? Were some of your ideas impractical? How did you and/or your church deal with these changes.) I don't know of anything that was a big surprise. I mean, no matter what your model of ministry, you are still dealing with people. Sinners, every one. So the challenges we have had are really not about the FIC model but about people not wanting to be held accountable (so they bolt) or about people not liking something that we would consider a non-essential (like the music styles), so they bolt. It's always exciting! Part of the problem is that we live in a consumer-driven culture and people drag that into the church.

All churches experience families or members that decide to leave the church for a variety of reasons. Have any families or members left your church as a result of your decision to move to a family-integrated/household model? For those that left, did you accept their "given" reason for leaving to be the true reason? If not, what are your thoughts regarding the other possible reasons that some may have left? As stated above, they have left for other reasons. Back in 1993-95, we may have lost 2-3 families because of the FIC model. Now most who come to the church come precisely *because* we are an FIC.

Have you had families join your church simply because of your household approach to ministry? Yes, as above.

Aside from a family's own children within your church, how many others have come to faith within the context of your church's ministry? There is obvious church growth when new families join (who are already Christian), or when numbers increase due to childbirth. What we are looking for here are the additions to your church in the past of new Christians, non-blood-related to currently attending families. There have been four adults come to Christ in the past two years.

For churches considering a move towards this vision of ministry, what special insights and/or practical suggestions would you share with them help them on their journey. Nothing that I have not already shared in this survey or written about in my book!

Please briefly state some short-term and long-term goals for your church.
Both goals are the same: to advance the Kingdom of God by planting other family-integrated churches and helping the people at Antioch grow and mature as followers of Jesus Christ.

Please share anything else you would like to share that you believe would be beneficial to those considering a move towards family-integrated/household ministry.

LaVergne, TN USA
21 October 2009

161606LV00001B/63/P